New York
Wish You Were Here!

CREATED BY
DIANA KRAUSE OLIVER

Schiffer Publishing Ltd
4880 Lower Valley Road • Atglen, PA 19310

Dedication

Dedicated to the memory of my father, Edward Krause, who treated every corner of Manhattan like a friend he had just met.

All photographs taken by the author.
Mosaic subway photos were taken as part of a grant from Art Matters, Inc. 1990 and exhibited at the New York Transit Museum.
Contributing Photo Editor: Maurice Dalton Oliver

Library of Congress Control Number: 2014940174

Designed by Matt Goodman
Type set in Stuyvesant, Bodega Serif & New Baskerville

ISBN: 978-0-7643-4589-0
Printed in The United States of America

Published by Schiffer Publishing, Ltd.
4880 Lower Valley Road
Atglen, PA 19310
Phone: (610) 593-1777; Fax: (610) 593-2002
E-mail: Info@schifferbooks.com

For our complete selection of fine books on this and related subjects, please visit our website at www.schifferbooks.com. You may also write for a free catalog.

This book may be purchased from the publisher. Please try your bookstore first.

We are always looking for people to write books on new and related subjects. If you have an idea for a book, please contact us at proposals@schifferbooks.com.

Schiffer Publishing's titles are available at special discounts for bulk purchases for sales promotions or premiums. Special editions, including personalized covers, corporate imprints, and excerpts can be created in large quantities for special needs. For more information, contact the publisher.

Special Thanks

With love to my New York husband Maurice, for his constant encouragement and photo editing support. To our Chicago son Omar, who makes anywhere we travel home.

To my mom Elsie Krause, for her adventurous Upper East Side attitude and editing magic.

To Brooklyn Mike Roveccio, who taught me the power of 10 and the secret to good meatballs.

In memory of Marshall Raibman, a true New Yorker, who shared in my subway mosaic quest.

Thanks to Schiffer Publishing and my editor, Tina Libby, for being the light at the end of my tunnel.

And to the generations of immigrants who came to call New York home.

Contents

City Hall,
Subway Station
New York.

Introduction

The sky was clear and blue on the morning of 9/11/2001. I was on an early United Airlines flight out of Chicago about to descend into New York for business. The plane seemed to stop in mid-air as everyone was ordered to their seats immediately. We were diverted to Philadelphia where we were ushered off the plane and locked into the airport. Cell phones didn't work, and all we could do was to watch television with the rest of the world as the horrific events of that morning unfolded. On that day the City, and the world, lost a sense of balance that changed our lives.

In 1988, while studying textiles, I traveled each day by subway from Queens to Parsons School of Design in downtown Manhattan. As the train passed each station, I began to notice its mosaics, and became fascinated with the variety of ceramic murals and plaques that were underground. At the time many of the subway stations were badly neglected and years of dirt, water damage, and graffiti had taken its toll. I thought someone needed to document these hidden works of art before time got the best of them. Once out of school and out of work, I decided that someone needed to be me.

I set out to create life-sized examples of the mosaics to show their intricate details and decided the best way to do this was to emboss an impression, tile by tile. With a roll of velum drafting paper and a box of Crayola® crayons, I headed out to capture Canal Street. My first challenge was to tape the paper up in between the rush of wind from passing trains. To reach the murals I brought a wooden crate which also acted as a chair when I got tired. Letter by letter I started to trace the tiles C-A-N-A-L.

The January cold chilled my bones. When a train would platform, I'd jump on and off before the doors closed, just to get warm. At one point, a woman stood behind me watching for quite some time. She asked why I was doing this. I told her of my interest in documenting the mosaics and that I was motivated by the word C-A-N. As she walked away, she said, "You know it also says A-N-A-L."

The Canal Street sign was 8 feet long. I would return a few more times before the whole sign was completely embossed. Back in my studio I taped the finished sign to a wall and painted it with black dye. The wax crayon resisted the dye and stained the background paper creating a stained glass-like-effect. I was hooked.

For the next few years I completed a collection of embossed murals that showed different styles used throughout the decades of subway expansion.

Spring Street is ornate with vines and flowers reflecting the Victorian style of the early 1900s.

Christopher Street reflects the arts and crafts period.

Pennsylvania Station is bold, streamlined, and modern, from the 1940s.

In the 1990s I received a grant from Art Matters, Inc. to photograph the additional mosaics I wanted to record. The New York Transit Museum in Brooklyn exhibited the murals and photographs in a show called "The Lost Mosaics of New York's Underground Subways."

My early interest in these mosaics led me to study the history of the subways and its effect on the expansion of the City of New York. Each station represented a community that grew above ground. To expand my photo collection I also started to document the City's neighborhoods, capturing what they looked like before the turn of the 21st century.

Through the 1990s, I worked as a textile designer in Midtown Manhattan, and traveled everywhere with my camera, taking pictures. Just before 2000, I was offered a design position in Chicago and moved away from the city I loved. Unable to continue to photograph New York, I started to collect antique postcards of the city, which made an interesting comparison to my pictures.

Years have gone by since I started my quest to document the subway mosaics and the neighborhoods of Manhattan. As time has passed, these photographs and postcards have only become more meaningful. There is no place in the world that can match the energy and excitement of New York City.

My collection is a love story to a city so dear to my heart. *New York: Wish You Were Here* shows a glimpse of yesterday that now seems so long ago.

Once Upon A Time . . .

During the last Ice Age, the entire upper Midwest, the area north of the Ohio River, and most of Canada were covered with a sheet of ice.

The island of Manhattan was formed when a glacier tore off the top of a mountain range (leaving what is now the New Jersey Palisades) and pushed land and rock out to the Atlantic Ocean. Evidence of this glacial movement can be traced on the rocks and boulders in Central Park.

Long Island and Staten Island were defined approximately 12,000 to 13,000 years ago when the waters of the Upper Bay broke through into the Lower Bay. A tidal strait called the Narrows connects the Hudson River to the Atlantic Ocean, creating a great harbor and a gateway to the City of New York.

Manhattan is made up of bedrock, and its strength allows for a strong foundation for the City's buildings. New York skyscrapers are concentrated in lower Manhattan and then again in the midtown area; it is under these areas that the most solid bedrock can be found.

On Arrival

Explorers

The area that is now Manhattan was once home to the Lenape Indians.

In the 1500s, it was the Lenape Indians in canoes who greeted Florentine Giovanni da Verrazano, the first European explorer to reach New York Harbor.

It was not until the 1600s when Henry Hudson, an Englishman who worked for the Dutch East India Company, explored the area up the river that would later bare his name, the Hudson River.

EMBARKATION OF THE PILGRIMS. FROM DELFT HAVEN. JULY 2[illegible] 520 48007

In the 1600s, European settlers and fur traders created two colonies; one on Governors Island called New Netherlands, and one on Manhattan Island called New Amsterdam. These settlers traded with the natives and started the North American fur trade.

Peter Minuit became the director of the New Netherlands. He is credited with acquiring the island of Manhattan in 1626 from the Lenape Indians in exchange for trade goods worth 60 guilders, often said to be worth 24 dollars. This actually amounts to approximately $1,000 in today's currency.

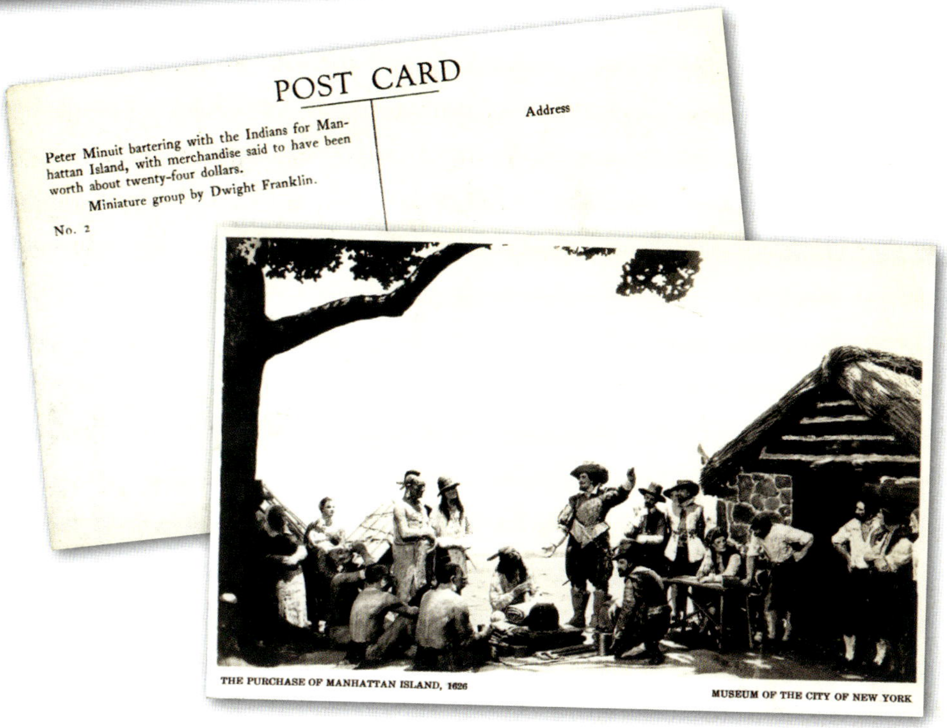

POST CARD

Address

Peter Minuit bartering with the Indians for Manhattan Island, with merchandise said to have been worth about twenty-four dollars.
Miniature group by Dwight Franklin.

No. 2

THE PURCHASE OF MANHATTAN ISLAND, 1626 MUSEUM OF THE CITY OF NEW YORK

CORNER OF EXCHANGE PLACE AND BROAD STREET, 1690 (FIRST IMPROVEMENT OF THE OLD SHEEP PASTURE).

New Amsterdam was formally incorporated as a city in 1653. In 1664, the British conquered it and renamed it New York.

Immigrants

American immigration history can be viewed in four periods: the colonial period, the mid-19th century, the turn of the 20th, and post-1965. Each phase brought distinct national groups, races, and ethnicities to the United States.

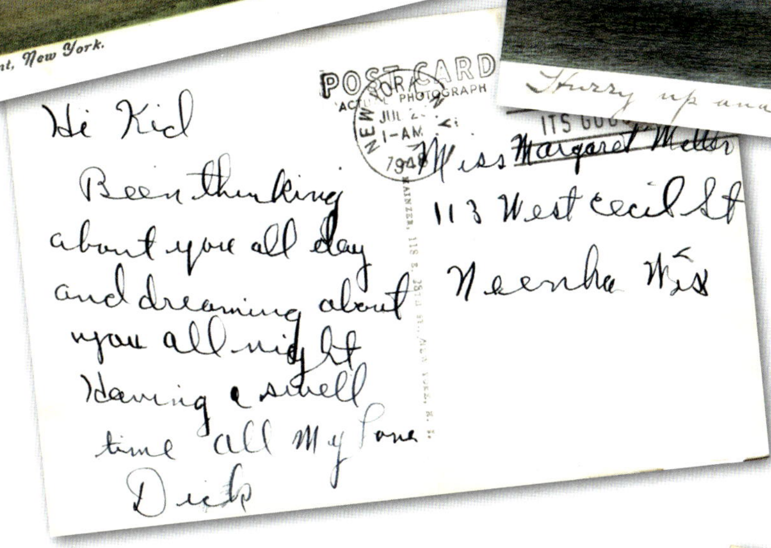

Some came for the adventure in a land of great opportunity where the Streets were said to be paved in gold. Others left their homeland just to survive.

Many immigrants flocked to neighborhoods where they could be among their own, creating strong ethnic communities throughout the boroughs of Manhattan.

Ellis Island

The main port of entry at Ellis Island opened in 1892 and processed 12 million arrivals to the United States.

The mid-nineteenth century saw an influx of immigrants from northern Europe. The early twentieth century immigration was mainly from Southern and Eastern Europe and in the 1960s, from Latin America and Asia.

The Statue of Liberty

"Give us your tired, your poor, your huddled masses yearning to breathe free"

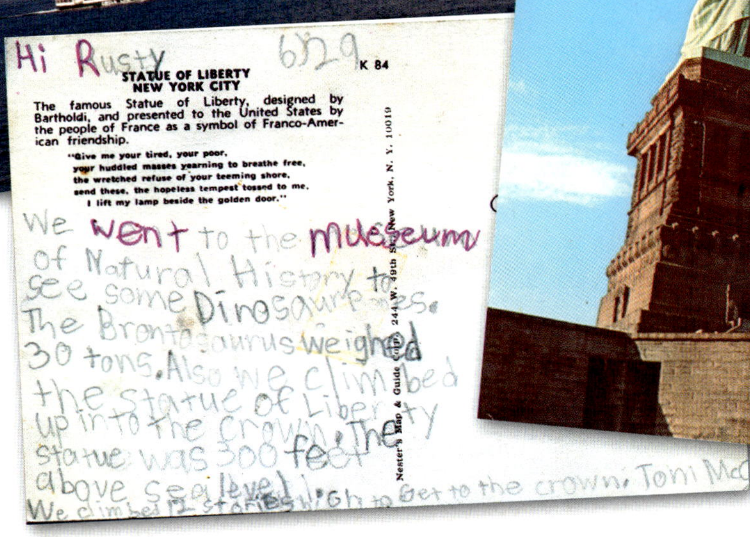
Hi Rusty 6/29 K 84

STATUE OF LIBERTY
NEW YORK CITY

The famous Statue of Liberty, designed by Bartholdi, and presented to the United States by the people of France as a symbol of Franco-American friendship.

"Give me your tired, your poor,
your huddled masses yearning to breathe free,
the wretched refuse of your teeming shore,
send these, the hopeless tempest tossed to me,
I lift my lamp beside the golden door."

Nester's Map & Guide Corp., 244 W. 49th St., New York, N. Y. 10019

We went to the museum of Natural History to see some Dinosaur bones. The Brontosaurus weighed 30 tons. Also we climbed the statue of Liberty up into the crown. The statue was 300 feet above sea level! We climbed 12 stories high to get to the crown. Toni Mc

A gift of friendship from the people of France to the people of the United States, it has become a universal symbol of freedom and democracy. The Statue of Liberty was dedicated in 1886, designated as a National Monument in 1924, and restored for her centennial in 1986.

Around Town Transportation

Ferry Service

Before the introduction of trains and automobiles, ferry service was the only way to get off the island.

Robert Fulton, an American engineer and inventor widely credited with improving steam navigation. The steamship operated from 1924 to 1971.

The Hudson River Day Line transported passengers along the Hudson River, between New York City and upstate to Albany.

Staten Island Ferry

A passenger ferry service that runs between Manhattan Island and Staten Island.

The ferry has been in service since 1905, and currently carries over 21 million passengers annually on a five mile journey.

The boats leave from South Ferry at the southernmost tip of Manhattan, near Battery Park. The area also has piers for ferries to Ellis Island, Liberty Island, and Governor's Island.

Bridges to Brooklyn

The Brooklyn Bridge

One of the oldest suspension bridges in the United States. Completed in 1883, it connects the boroughs of Manhattan and Brooklyn by spanning the East River.

The bridge originally was designed to carry horse-drawn carriages, trolley cars, elevated trains, and included a pedestrian walkway.

The elevated train lines were discontinued in 1944. In 1950, the streetcars also stopped, and the bridge was rebuilt to carry six lanes of automobile traffic. Due to the roadway's height restrictions, commercial vehicles and buses are prohibited from using this bridge.

To anticipate any structural stress, the bridge was designed with three separate systems of support; a suspension system, a diagonal stay system, and a stiffening truss.

Following the 1965 and 1977 blackouts, and especially after the September 11, 2001 attacks on the World Trade Center, the bridge was used by millions of people leaving Manhattan.

The massive number of people using this bridge could never have been anticipated by the original designer, John Augustus Roebling.

The Williamsburg Bridge

The bridge opened in 1903, at a cost of $24,200,000, yet no tolls have ever been charged for motor vehicles to use it. The tracks in the center of the bridge were initially used by the Brooklyn Rapid Transit Company elevated railroad. Today, the tracks are used by the New York City subways.

Crossing the East River, the bridge connects the Lower East Side of Manhattan at Delancey Street with the Williamsburg section of Brooklyn.

The Manhattan Bridge

Is the last of the three suspension bridges built across the lower East River. The bridge opened in 1909, and was designed by Leon Moisseiff.

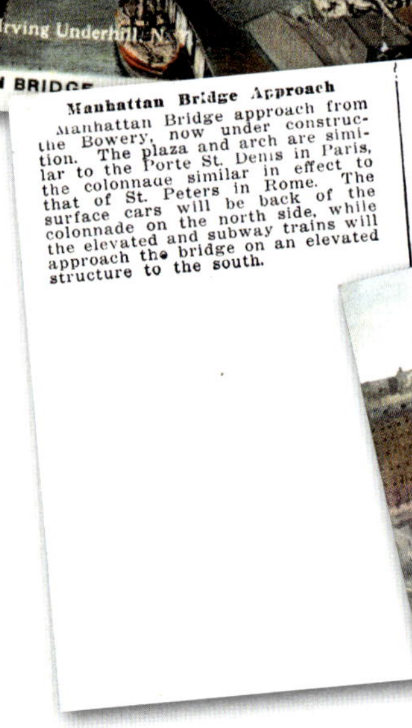

The bridge connects lower Manhattan at Canal Street with Brooklyn at Flatbush Avenue.

The New Manhattan Bridge, New-York.

The neighborhood under the bridge on the Brooklyn side is referred to as DUMBO, an acronym for Down Under the Manhattan Bridge Overpass.

In the 1970s, the area became primarily residential, when artists seeking relatively large and inexpensive loft apartment spaces for studios and homes began moving there. New residents coined the acronym DUMBO in the belief such an unattractive name would help deter developers.

Near the end of the 20th century, as property became more and more expensive in Manhattan, DUMBO has grown to become an important arts center. It is now a model for similar waterfront developments.

The four subway tracks on the bridge are used by the New York City subway. For 18 years, between 1986 and 2004, one set of tracks (or the other set) was closed to repair structural damage.

The Verrazano-Narrows Bridge

Named for both the Italian explorer Giovanni da Verrazano—the first known European navigator to enter New York Harbor and the Hudson River—and the Narrows, the body of water it spans.

It was the longest suspension bridge in the world when completed in 1964, and is still the longest bridge span in the Americas.

The bridge is a double-decked suspension bridge that connects the boroughs of Staten Island to Brooklyn.

The Verrazano-Narrows Bridge is the gateway to New York Harbor. All cruise ships and container ships arriving at the Port of New York and New Jersey must pass underneath and must be built to accommodate the clearance.

Ocean Liners

The "golden age" of ocean liners spans from the beginning of the 20th century to the end of World War II. Driven by the strong demand of European immigration, ocean liners were the primary mode of travel until the 1960s when airliners took to the sky.

Train Travel

With every new expansion in transportation, the boundaries of the city of New York exploded with new neighborhoods and communities.

"How New York Grew: Subways, Neighborhoods and People"

The New York Transit Museum

Elevated Railway

The first "EL" started operating in 1870 and traveled along Greenwich Street and Ninth Avenue. Later lines were built on Second, Third, and Sixth Avenues.

The steam-powered elevated railroads lasted about 80 years. Built over major avenues, their heavy presence darkened the Streets below with shadow and soot. By the 1950s, most of the elevated structures were demolished.

Underground Trains

By the 1860s, traffic in New York was a nightmare, especially along Broadway. Inventor Alfred Ely Beach was the one of a few visionaries who proposed building an underground railway to help relieve the traffic congestion. In 1870, based on the principles of pneumatic tubes (used to transport letters and packages), Beach constructed a tunnel under Broadway and built a small passenger railway that ran for three years.

During the same time, other investors built an elevated railway along Greenwich Street and Ninth Avenue, which operated with a small steam engine. The idea of underground transportation was met with great political resistance while the elevated rail lines were more popularly endorsed.

The Great Blizzard of 1888 dumped 40 inches of snow on the Metropolitan region and stopped the City completely. The need for underground transportation became more critical.

The Subways

In 1898, New York, Kings, Richmond, and parts of Queens and Westchester Counties were incorporated into the City of Greater New York. During this era the expanded City resolved that the future of rapid transit was to be underground.

The Interborough Rapid Transit Company, or IRT (which at the time ran the elevated lines in Manhattan), was contracted to build and operate the subways, sharing the profits with the City and guaranteeing a fixed five cent fare.

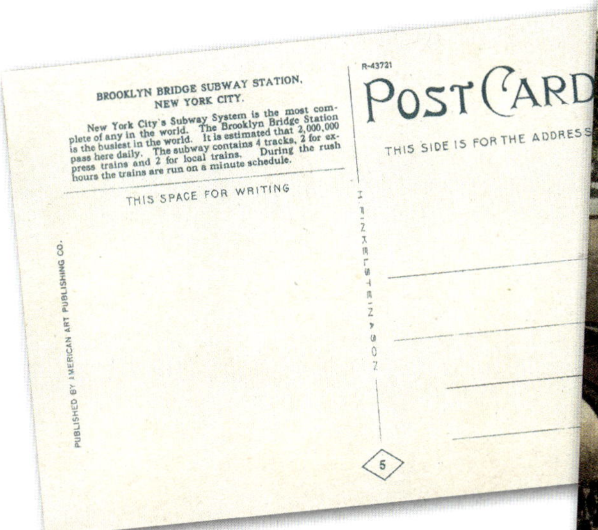

The first underground line of the subway opened in 1904, connecting the island of Manhattan to Brooklyn, City Hall Station.

By the 1920s, the Brooklyn-Manhattan Transit Corporation, or BMT, operated the majority of the rapid transit and streetcar lines in Brooklyn, with extensions into Queens and Manhattan.

In the 1940s, the transportation assets of the IRT and BMT systems were taken over by the City of New York.

In 1953, the New York City Transit Authority incorporated to combine all transportation under what is now known to the public as MTA New York City Transit.

The Hudson Terminal and Tubes

Opened in 1909 to connect Manhattan to New Jersey.

Built by the Hudson and Manhattan Railroad, the terminal was an engineering marvel of its time. Planned and designed with a series of ramps descending from the street level to the mezzanine, it allowed pedestrian traffic to flow in and out of the station quickly and easily.

By 1922, 60 million passengers annually passed through the system.

In the late 1950s, the Hudson Terminal was torn down by the Port Authority to make way for plans to build a "World Trade Center." The Port Authority Trans-Hudson (PATH) rapid transit system would use the same cast iron tubes under the Hudson River to bring commuters into Lower Manhattan.

Automobiles and Tunnels

The Model T Ford was the first mass-produced passenger vehicle in America. It ushered in the 1900s, the century of the automobile, and dramatically changed the landscape of the country.

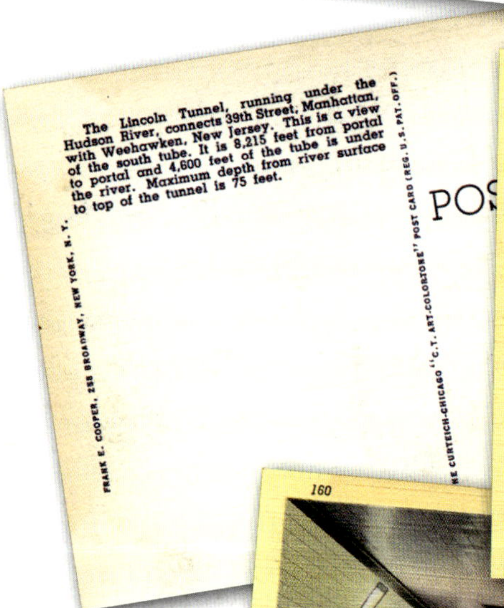

The Holland Tunnel, completed in 1927, along with The Lincoln Tunnel, 1937, are highways that tunnel under the Hudson River connecting Manhattan with New Jersey.

The Queens Midtown Tunnel opened in the 1940s to connect Manhattan under the East River to the borough of Queens, and to Long Island.

After World War II, Long Island became the fastest growing suburb in the United States, thanks in part to the automobile.

Air Travel

Zeppelins, the hydrogen-filled rigid airships that were popular in the 1930s, were one of the first transatlantic passenger airlines.

The first intercontinental trip was in 1928 from Germany to New Jersey, and took over four days.

The Art Deco spire of the Empire State Building was originally designed to serve as a dirigible terminal for the zeppelins and other airships. The building created such updrafts that docking there became dangerous and impractical.

The Hindenburg disaster in 1937, along with political and economic issues, hastened the demise of the zeppelin.

Airplanes

In 1927, aviator Charles Lindbergh made the first transatlantic, nonstop flight from Roosevelt Field in Long Island to Paris.

Not long after, Pan American World Airways, or Pan Am, began scheduling international flights.

Airports

Newark Airport was the first major airport to service New York City.

The initiative to develop an airport for commercial flights to New York came from then Mayor Fiorello La Guardia. When his TWA flight to New York landed in Newark (New Jersey), he ordered the plane to be flown to Brooklyn's Floyd Bennett Field. Giving an impromptu press conference to reporters along the way, he urged New Yorkers to support a new airport within their city limits.

Construction started in 1937 on what was the site of the Gala Amusement Park, owned by the Steinway piano company.

By the 1940s, Laguardia Airport became insufficient to handle the increased demand in air traffic. Construction for a new international airport began along the Queens/Brooklyn border.

JFK Airport was originally known as Idlewild Airport after the Idlewild Golf Course that it displaced. It was renamed the John F. Kennedy International Airport in 1963, one month after the President was assassinated.

Downtown
East Side — West Side

New York City Hall

City Hall officially opened in 1812. It is the oldest City Hall in the United States that still houses its original governmental functions.

Located at the center of City Hall Park in the Civic Center between Broadway, Park Row, and Chambers Street.

The historic Blue Room is where New York City mayors have been giving official press conferences for decades and is often used for bill-signing ceremonies.

The steps of City Hall frequently provide a backdrop for political demonstrations and press conferences concerning city politics.

Skyscrapers

In the 18th century, the term skyscraper was used to describe the tallest mast on a ship. Later the name was given to the buildings of Manhattan that grew towards the sky.

When the Eiffel Tower was built in 1889 in Paris, it taunted American capitalists to build taller buildings in New York City. By 1909, the Metropolitan Life Tower rose to 50 stories high, followed by the Woolworth Building in 1913 at 57 stories, and soon surpassed by the Bank of Manhattan Building in 1929 at 71 stories.

Steel and glass framed skyscrapers changed the skylines of cities like New York and Chicago.

Battery Park

A 25-acre public park located at the southern tip of Manhattan Island, overlooking the New York harbor.

AQUARIUM AND BATTERY PARK, New York City. The Aquarium, formerly known as Castle Garden Fort, is located at the foot of Battery Park, and is open to the public daily from 9 A. M. to 5. P. M. Here can be seen in large glass tanks the most valuable and complete collection of fish, seals, turtles and other deep sea inhabitants in existence. At the entrance of the harbor is the Statue of Liberty and a little further up is Ellis Island, through which all immigrants landing in New York City must pass.

Copyright American Studio, New York.

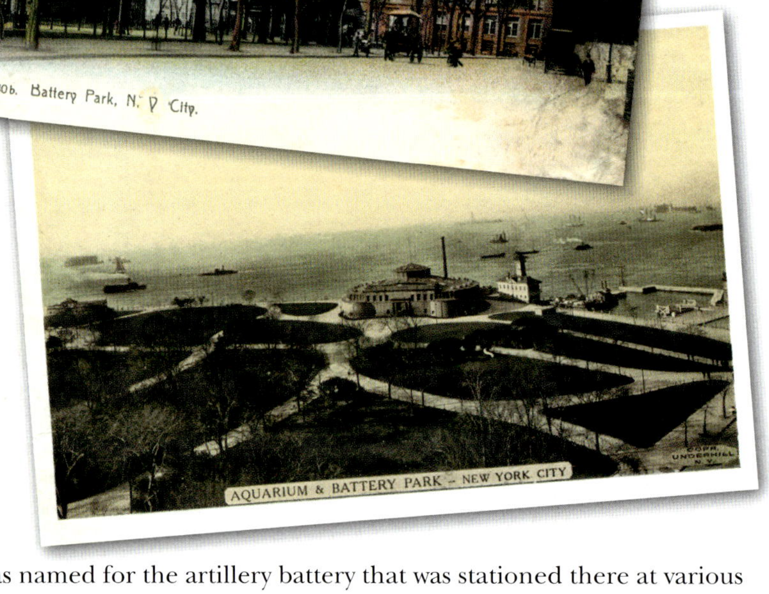

It was named for the artillery battery that was stationed there at various times by the Dutch and British in order to protect the settlements behind it.

Along the waterfront, ferries depart for the Statue of Liberty, Ellis Island, and Staten Island. Under the park there are tunnels carrying traffic to Brooklyn, the FDR Drive, and the IRT subway lines.

Battery Park includes memorials and monuments to American veterans, firefighters, victims of the AIDS epidemic, and those who died on 9/11.

Battery Park City, a planned community, was built on landfill in the 1970s and '80s. It includes Robert F. Wagner Park and the Battery Park City Promenade.

US Customs House

Across State Street to the northeast of Battery Park. Completed in 1907, the Customs House was one of the earliest designations of the New York City Landmark's Preservation Commission. In the 1970s, the building was saved from demolition.

The Beaux-Arts building now houses a branch of the National Museum of the American Indians and the district U.S. Bankruptcy Court.

Bowling Green

A small public park at the foot of Broadway, next to the site of the original Dutch fort of New Amsterdam. Once used for bowling, it is the oldest public park in New York City and is still surrounded by its original 18th-century fence.

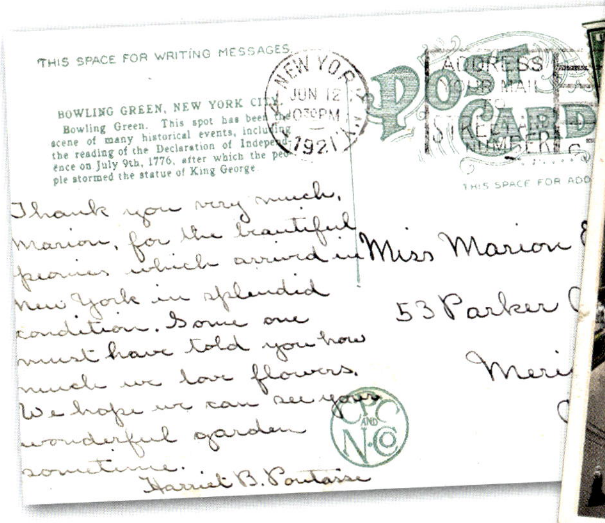

The park suffered neglect after World War II; it was restored by the city in the 1970s. Bowling Green is known as the "Canyon of Heroes" as it marks the origination point for the ticker-tape parades.

At the northern end of the park is a bronze sculpture of a charging bull, which has become the recognizable symbol for the Financial District.

The Financial District

Wall Street

In the 17th century, the Dutch built a 12-foot stockade wall to protect the settlement of New Amsterdam against attacks from various Native American Indian tribes.

The origin of the New York Stock Exchange goes back to the late 18th century, when the Buttonwood Agreement was signed by a group of stock brokers under a buttonwood tree on Wall Street.

By 1817, the organization drafted a constitution and renamed itself the "New York Stock & Exchange Board."

Broad Street

was originally an inlet from the East River named Broad Canal.

The street witnessed major changes as life progressed from Dutch to British rule and finally American independence.

In 1835, the Great Fire of New York destroyed over 500 properties, including whatever historical buildings were left from the early times.

Federal Hall and Wall Street

was the scene of the United States' first presidential inauguration.

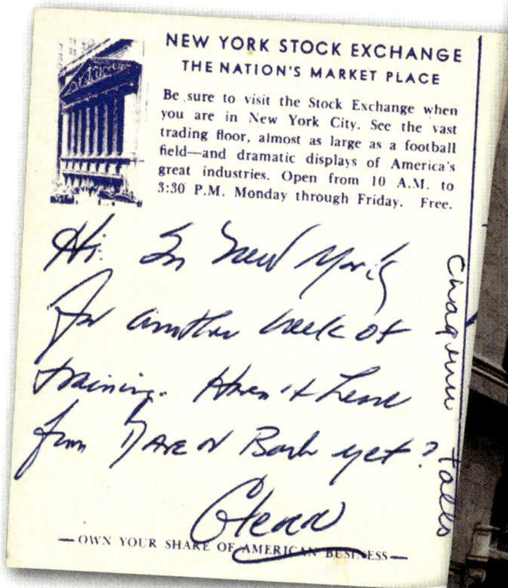

George Washington took the oath of office on the balcony of Federal Hall overlooking Wall Street on April 30, 1789.

Trinity Church

In the 1690s, Governor Benjamin Fletcher approved the purchase of land in Lower Manhattan by the Church of England for construction of a church. The structure burnt down in 1776. A second structure was built and torn down after being damaged in a winter storm.

The third Trinity Church was finished in 1846 and at the time of its completion its 281 foot spire and cross was the highest point in New York. It was surpassed in 1890 by the New York World Building.

The burial grounds of Trinity Churchyard, at Wall Street and Broadway, include famous historic figures such as Alexander Hamilton, William Bradford, Robert Fulton, and Captain James Lawrence.

New York Stock Exchange

Originally called the "curb market" because brokers traded on the Streets, the AMEX has been at the forefront of the U.S. financial markets over the past two centuries.

Black Tuesday, October 29, 1929, saw the collapse of the US stock market, which ushered in the Great Depression.

With construction of the World Trade Center in the 1970s, the Financial District shifted from Wall Street to the Trade Center complex.

The World Trade Center

Groundbreaking for the World Trade Center took place in 1966. The North Tower and the South Tower were completed in 1970 and 1971, respectively.

The construction project involved excavating a massive amount of material ,which was used as landfill to create Battery Park City.

The World Trade Center was designed by Minoru Yamaski in the early 1960s, using a tube-frame structural design for the twin 110-story towers. The project was part of the Port Authority of New York and New Jersey merger to take over the Hudson & Manhattan Railroad, which became the Port Authority Trans-Hudson. The PATH ran under the Twin Towers, connecting Lower Manhattan to New Jersey.

The World Trade Center was a complex of seven buildings in Lower Manhattan. The Twin Towers became a symbol of American capitalism.

On September 11, 2001, terrorists attacked and demolished both buildings by flying a jet plane into each of the towers.

In honor of the thousands of lives lost on that day, the site is being rebuilt to include five new skyscrapers, a national memorial and museum, a transportation hub, retail space, and a performing arts center.

South Street Seaport

The seaport is just south of the Brooklyn Bridge, located where Fulton Street meets the East River and adjacent to the Financial District. The area became a vital commercial center with warehouses, markets, and taverns. By the mid-1860s, many shipping lines left this port for larger ones situated up the Hudson River. The area was almost completely deserted for decades.

Adjacent to the Seaport, the Fulton Fish Market was one of the largest wholesale markets in the world. It operated for 183 years on this waterfront until relocating in 2005 to Hunts Point in the Bronx.

TONTINE COFFEE-HOUSE.

In 1967, the South Street Seaport Museum opened helping to preserve the historic importance of the area. The Seaport is now a designated historic district, featuring the largest concentration of restored early 19th-century commercial buildings in the City.

OLD COFFEE-HOUSE AND COFFEE-HOUSE SLIP.

Renovation include original mercantile buildings known as Schermerhorn Row, sailing ships, and Pier 17 Pavilion, which features restaurants and retail shopping.

Fraunces Tavern

Originally built as a home for the wealthy Delancey family, Fraunces Tavern was sold to and renamed for its Revolutionary War-era proprietor, Samuel Fraunces. Located on the corner of Pearl and Broad Streets, it is one of Manhattan's oldest surviving buildings, dating from 1671.

After British troops evacuated New York, the tavern hosted an elaborate "turtle feast" dinner on December 4, 1783, in the building's Long Room for U.S. General George Washington, where he bade farewell to his officers of the Continental Army.

The Lower East Side

Originally the area alongside the East River from approximately the Manhattan Bridge and Canal Street, up to 14th Street and Broadway. It included areas known today as the East Village, Alphabet City, Chinatown, Bowery, and Little Italy.

The Lower East Side is one of the oldest neighborhoods of the City. For many years, it was a poor and ethnically diverse area.

It is perhaps best known as having once been the center of Jewish culture. During the early part of the 20th century, Second Avenue was known as the "Yiddish Broadway."

The area became home to many newly arriving immigrants: Irish, Polish, Ukrainian, and German. Today it is predominantly Hispanic and Asian.

In the second half of the 1990s, the neighborhood saw an influx of yuppies. Storefront shops and galleries are being crowded out making room for expensive retail boutiques, trendy restaurants, and bars.

The Bowery

THE BOWERY HOUSE.

The Bowery is the oldest thoroughfare in the City. Once a Lenape Indian footpath, it spanned roughly the entire length of the island, from north to south. The community took its name from the old Dutch word *bouwerij*, meaning "farm."

From 1878 to 1955, the Third Avenue EL ran from Bowery to the Bronx.

By the 1890s, the Bowery became the center for prostitution, saloons, dance halls, gay bars, tattoo parlors, and cheap lodging for the down and out.

In the early 1920s, a major effort to develop retail space brought in restaurant supply stores, a few of which are still there today.

From the 1940s through the 1970s, the Bowery became known as "Skid Row," notable for the "Bowery Bums," alcoholics and the homeless who slept on the Streets.

Since the 1990s, the entire Lower East Side has been reviving with high-rise condominiums.

Canal Street

Canal Street was once literally an active canal until the 1820s when it was filled to create a street. It cuts east and west, joining New Jersey via the Holland Tunnel to Brooklyn via the Manhattan Bridge.

In the early 20th century, the jewelry trade centered on the corner of Canal and Bowery, but moved in the mid-century to the current Diamond District on 47th Street.

The area around Canal Street was also previously the home for garment factories, warehouses, and stores selling surplus and salvage.

The proximity of the fashion industry has kept some garment work in the local area, though today almost all of the garment industry has moved overseas.

Today, vendors on Canal Street sell imitation perfumes, watches, and handbags, and are notorious for counterfeit name-brand merchandise.

For many years, Canal Street separated Chinatown from Little Italy. It also is the northern boundary of the neighborhood of Tribeca and the southern boundary of SoHo.

Chinatown

Chinese immigrants faced with increasing discrimination on the West Coast, moved to East Coast cities in search of employment. They settled in this area and opened hand laundries and restaurants.

Chinatown started on Mott, Park, Pell and Doyers Streets, east of the notorious Five Points District. The early days of Chinatown were dominated by Chinese "tongs," or secret societies, which were often tied to criminal activity.

In the 1960s, immigration quotas were lifted, allowing for an influx of Asian immigrants. By the 1990s, Chinatown expanded as its people moved into other parts of the Lower East Side.

Currently, rising real-estate prices are also affecting Chinatown. Unable to afford Manhattan rents, Asian communities have expanded to Flushing, Queens, and Sunset Park, Brooklyn.

Five Points

Five Points was a notorious slum centered on the five-cornered intersection of what is now Park, Worth, and Baxter Streets, located about halfway between what is now Chinatown and the Financial District.

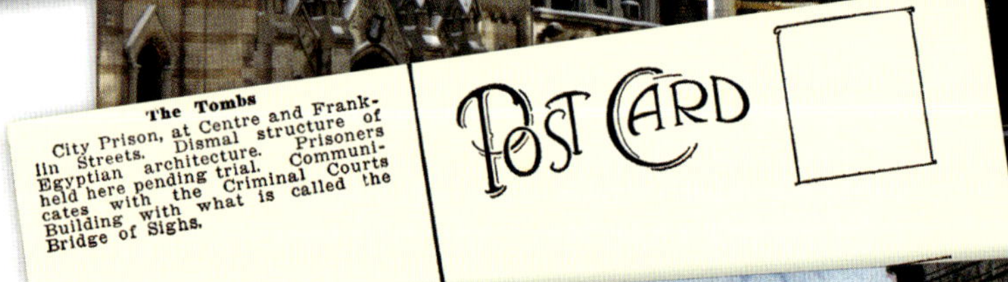

Rival gangs fighting for their turf amid desperately poor conditions made the area one of the most dangerous. At one time it had the highest murder rate of any slum in the world.

In the early 1800s, poor Irish immigrants, most of whom were refugees from the Great Famine, settled in the area.

In the late 1800s, the slums were leveled and replaced by state administration buildings, criminal courts, and the notorious city prison, known as the Tombs.

Tribeca

The neighborhood on the Lower West Side gets its name from the first letters of the words "triangle below Canal." In the 19th and early 20th centuries, the neighborhood was a commercial center for the trade and manufacturing of textiles.

By the 1960s, Tribeca's industrial base had all but vanished. Empty commercial space attracted many artists to the area in the 1970s, much like SoHo and the Cast Iron Historic District.

The Tribeca Film Center was established with help from Robert De Niro; to contribute to the long-term recovery of Lower Manhattan after 9/11. Tribeca is now a thriving community known for its celebrity residents and as a backdrop for filming movies and television.

Little Italy

Southern Italian immigrants dominated the community centered on Mulberry Street, which was named for the trees that once grew there. Little Italy once extended from Canal Street on the south, to Bleecker on the north, west to Lafayette, and east to the Bowery.

By the 20th century, almost 90 percent of New York City's public works employees were Italian

Throughout most of the 1900s, powerful members of the Italian mafia families operated out of social clubs and restaurants in the neighborhood.

Many Italians achieved financial prosperity, which allowed them to leave the cramped apartments for more space in the outer boroughs of Staten Island, Brooklyn, and Queens.

By 2000, much of the neighborhood had been absorbed by Chinatown. Today the section of Mulberry Street between Broome and Canal is lined with a few Italian restaurants —all that is left of the Old Italian neighborhood.

Little Italy is known for the annual Feast of San Gennaro that celebrates the Patron Saint of Naples. Every September Mulberry Street is blocked off from traffic to make way for the festival.

The Villages

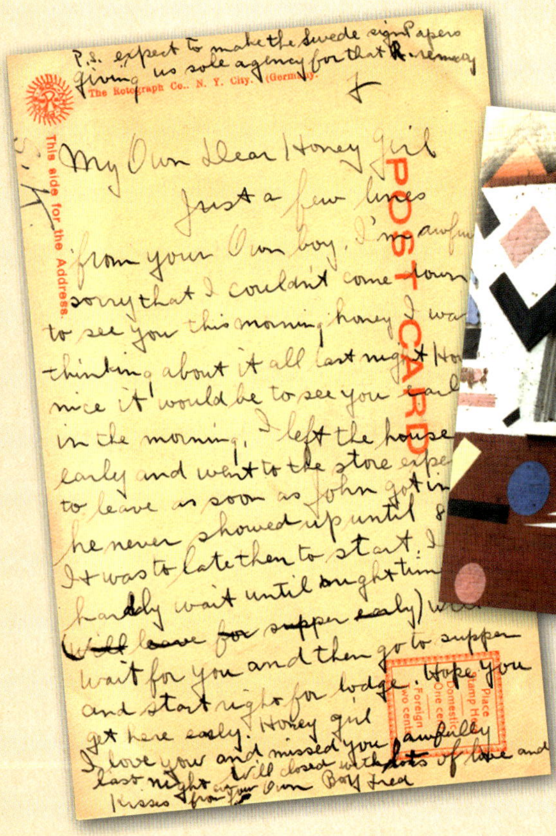

Manhattan is a city made up of small villages. When immigrants came to this country, they would seek out their own people and move into the same community. Each neighborhood had its unique language, religion, and culture. The spirit of a city is about constant change; nothing stays the same. Today, neighborhoods are totally mixed and only a few ethnic pockets remain.

Houston Street is dividing line between SoHo (south of Houston) and NoHo (north of Houston).

The original street was widened from Sixth Avenue to Essex Street in the early 1930s during construction of the Independent Subway System, or the IND.

From the 1940s to the 1960s, plans were in effect to level the community to make room for the Lower Manhattan Expressway. The highway was intended to ease traffic by connecting the Williamsburg Bridge on the east with the Holland Tunnel on the west.

SoHo & NoHo

Artist Lofts

To make room for the elevated highway, 14 city blocks would have had to be leveled. Community activists fought hard to save the neighborhood.

By the 1970s, manufacturing and commerce had vacated the area, leaving the community abandoned.

Artists who valued the large loft spaces, large windows, and cheap rents moved in. Most of these lofts were used illegally as living space, being neither zoned nor equipped for residential use.

The Cast Iron Historic District

The area is prized for its architectural elements. Cast iron was used for its fire-resistant properties and tensile strength, making it possible to erect large building facades at less cost than comparable stone fronts.

The pattern of gentrification is typically known as the "SoHo effect" and has been observed in cities around the United States. Struggling artists move in and improve an area with boutiques, restaurants, and galleries; the improved neighborhoods then command higher rents, forcing the artists to relocate.

Washington Square Park

The park is the heart of Greenwich Village and covers less then 10 acres. Once marshlands, the area has been used as farmland to feed the Dutch settlers, a potter's field after the Revolutionary War, and a site used for public execrations, protests and parades. It became a park in 1827, and was remodeled in the 1870s after the landscape of Central Park.

The fountain originally stood at the entrance to Central Park at 59th Street. The arch was built in 1892, and was modeled after the Arc de Triomphe in Paris. It became a fashionable address for the wealthy to build their mansions before they moved uptown.

Washington Place was the site of the Triangle Shirtwaist factory fire that killed 146 garment workers in 1911. The fire led to legislation requiring improved factory safety standards and helped spur the growth of the International Ladies' Garment Workers' Union.

Most of the buildings surrounding Washington Square Park now belong to NYU. The park has become the center of campus life.

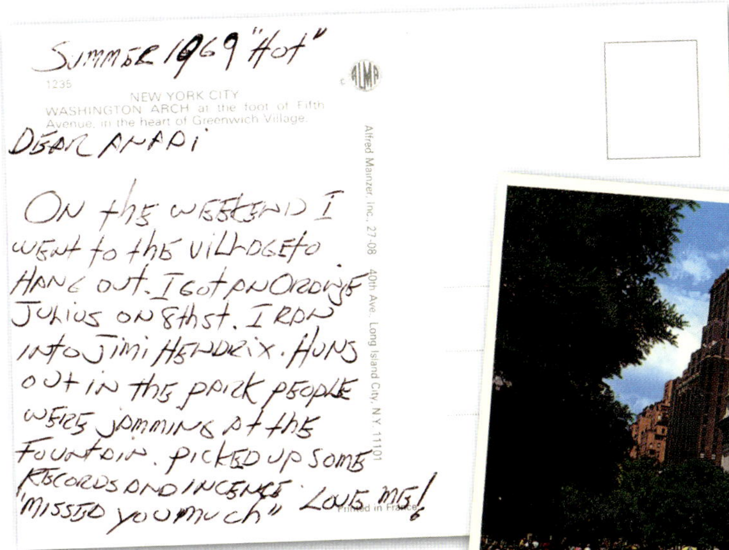
SUMMER 1969 "HOT"

1235

NEW YORK CITY
WASHINGTON ARCH at the foot of Fifth Avenue, in the heart of Greenwich Village.

ALMA

Alfred Mainzer, Inc., 27-08 40th Ave. Long Island City, N.Y. 11101

DEAR ANDI

ON THE WEEKEND I WENT TO THE VILLAGE TO HANG OUT. I GOT AN ORANGE JULIUS ON 8th ST. I RAN INTO JIMI HENDRIX. HUNG OUT IN THE PARK PEOPLE WERE JAMMING AT THE FOUNTAIN. PICKED UP SOME RECORDS AND INCENSE "MISSED YOU MUCH" LOVE, ME!

Printed in France

In the 1950s, Robert Moses planned to extend Fifth Avenue right through the park. For three decades, local activists fought—and won—to save their community.

The fountain has always been a gathering spot: in the 1940s and '50s for folk-singers and beat poets, and for hippies and anti-Vietnam protests in the late '60s and early '70s.

Today, street performers, comics, fire-eaters, dancers, and skaters entertain the crowds.

Greenwich Village

By the 1950s, "The Village" was the center of the bohemian culture. Writers, poets, artists, and students, known as the Beat Generation, moved here, fleeing from what they saw as oppressive social conformity. Regulars include Allen Ginsberg, Jack Kerouac, Jackson Pollack, and William de Kooning.

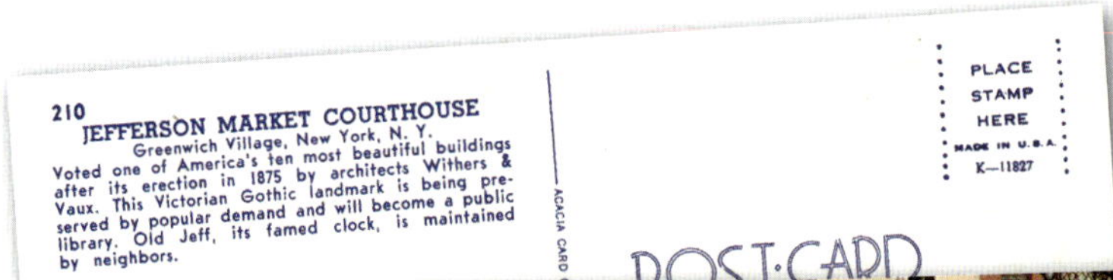

In the 1960s, the residents of the Village fought to preserve the architectural and historical integrity of the neighborhood. The Jefferson Market courthouse and women's prison is today the Jefferson Market Library.

In the '60s, clubs like the Village Gate, Bitter End, Village Vanguard, Café Wha?, and Folk City made the area a center for popular music. Miles Davis, Bob Dylan, and Jimmy Hendrix made the Village the place to be.

Today, no struggling artist could afford to live here.

Christopher Street

In 1961, Jane Jacobs, an area resident and author of *The Death and Life of Great American Cities,* headed a group that successfully stopped Mayor Robert Wagner's plan to demolish twelve blocks in the area that had been slated for "urban renewal."

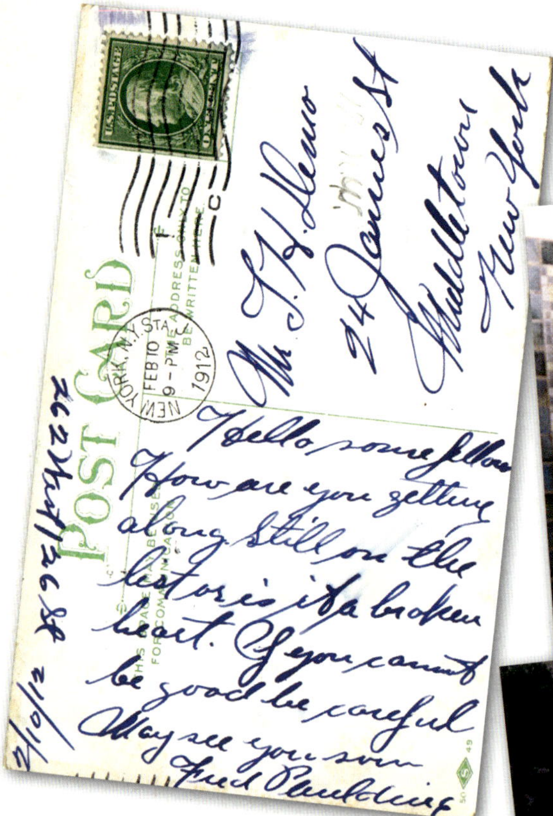

Christopher Street in the West Village is the site of the Stonewall riots of 1969, which are considered the start of the gay liberation movement of the 1970s. Today the street is a symbol of gay pride.

Meatpacking District

In 1900, Gansevoort Market was home to slaughterhouses and packing plants. In the 1930s, the West Side Line connected freight trains directly with factories and warehouses. By the early 1980s, the industrial area was abandoned by night, creating a haven for drug dealers, transsexuals, and prostitution.

As New York's arts community moved from SoHo to West Chelsea in the 1990s, the area has become one of the global centers for contemporary art. It runs between 10th and 11th Avenues from 18th to 28th Street.

Today's High Line Park is built on what remains of the old elevated tracks. The park runs from Gansevoort Street in the Meatpacking District through West Chelsea, Clinton/Hell's Kitchen, and will extend to the West Side Rail Yards north of 30th Street. It has quickly become a major tourist destination.

Chelsea

The neighborhood of Chelsea is primarily residential, roughly between 14th Street and 30th Street, and between 6th Avenue and the Hudson River.

Chelsea was a center for the motion picture industry before World War I. Since 1914, numerous movies and television shows have been produced in Chelsea studios.

This Gothic Revival building on 6th Avenue was constructed in 1845 as an Episcopal Church. From 1983 until 2007, the church was utilized as a nightclub called the Limelight: currently it is a marketplace.

The Chelsea Hotel, built in the 1880s, was New York's first cooperative apartment complex. The hotel has been the home of a number of prominent artists, musicians, writers, and philosophers.

Along the Hudson River, the Chelsea Piers were the City's primary luxury cruise terminals until 1935. The area was converted in 1994 to become the Chelsea Piers Sports & Entertainment Complex.

The East Village

In the 1900s, it was considered part of the Lower East Side, home to Eastern European Jews, Irish, and Italian immigrants.

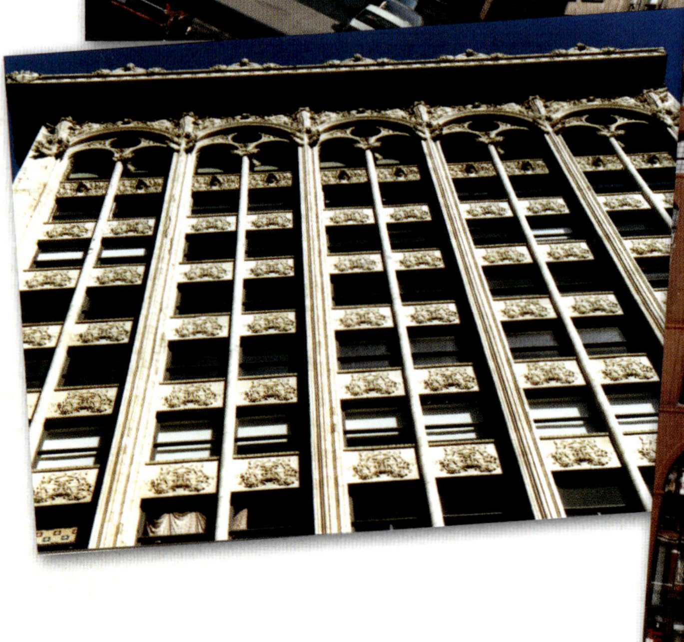

In the 1950s and '60s, beatniks, hippies, and artists moved into the neighborhood for cheap rent. The area was dubbed the "East Village" to distinguish it from the slums of the Lower East Side.

Alphabet City

Comprises nearly two-thirds of the East Village and was once a dangerous neighborhood. It gets its name from Avenues A, B, C, and D—the only Avenues in Manhattan to have single-letter names.

The area originally ended at the East River, where Avenue C is now located. Landfill, including World War II debris and rubble shipped from London, was used to extend the shoreline outward to provide the foundation for the Franklin D. Roosevelt Drive.

Cooper Union

The Cooper Union for the Advancement of Science and Art, commonly referred to simply as Cooper Union. It is located at Cooper Square and Astor Place.

Founded in 1859, the school established a radical new model of American higher education. Its mission reflects founder Peter Cooper's belief that education of the highest quality should be "free as air and water" and therefore available to all who qualify, independent of race, religion, sex, and social status.

Astor Place

John Jacob Astor, the first multi-millionaire in the United States, made his fortune on the trading of beaver fur and opium. He later diversified into New York real estate. After retiring, Astor spent the rest of his life as a patron to the arts.

In the mid-to-late 19th century, the area around Astor Place was home to many of the wealthiest New Yorkers, including members of the Astor, Vanderbilt, and Delano families.

By the turn of the 20th century, warehouses and manufacturing firms moved in and the elite moved uptown.

The neighborhood fell into disrepair until the late 1960s and '70s when it was revitalized. It has become a center of the counterculture in New York, and the birthplace of many Avant-guard art movements.

Union Square

The Square is named for the union of two major thoroughfares—where Broadway and the former Bowery Road, now 4th Avenue, come together.

In the late 1920s, Union Square Park was completely demolished to accommodate a new underground concourse for the subway.

In the 1970s, the Greenmarket program was established. It provides regional small farmers an opportunity to sell their produce at open-air markets in the City. The most famous is the Union Square Greenmarket.

Union Square has always been a popular meeting place given its central location in Manhattan and its connection to many subway lines.

In the days and weeks following the September 11, 2001, terrorist attacks, Union Square became a primary public gathering point. Mourners held candlelight vigils and created photographic memorials to honor the missing victims.

The Flatiron District

The area takes its name from the famous Flatiron Building designed by Daniel Burnham; when constructed in 1902, it was one of the tallest buildings in the city.

The building sits on a triangle of land formed by Fifth Avenue, Broadway, and East 22nd Street, with 23rd Street to the north.

It is said that the wind on 23rd Street, caused by the building's location and triangular shape, produced gusts strong enough to lift a woman's skirt. In the early 20th century, men would loiter on the street for a glimpse of stocking. To move the voyeurs along, the police would shout, "Hey you, 23 skidoo!"

Madison Square Park

The area has been a park since the 1680s. It was later named after the 4th President of the United States, James Madison. It is probably best known around the world for providing the name of Madison Square Garden. The sports arena was located just northeast of the park for 47 years until 1925.

Gramercy Park

Early in the 1800s, the area was in the middle of a swamp, which was later drained and filled. In 1833, a park was created by constructing a fence around a two-acre lot with landscaping and pathways. Beautiful surrounding Victorian townhouses would create a neighborhood that hasn't changed in years.

Gramercy Park is one of only two private parks in New York City. It is reserved for residents around the park who pay an annual fee to have an entrance key. The locks are changed yearly.

The neighborhood's boundaries are roughly 14th to 23rd Street; First Avenue to the east and Park Avenue south to the west.

Pete's Tavern, on 18th Street is one of New York's oldest surviving saloons, operating since 1864. It is where O. Henry wrote *The Gift of the Magi.* The tavern survived prohibition disguised as a flower shop.

Midtown

East Side

The Waldorf-Astoria Hotel

The original hotel, built in the 1890s, was the grandest luxury hotel in the world, and one of the first to offer room service.

By the 1920s, with so many new technological advances, it had become outdated. It was torn down in 1929 to make room for the Empire State Building.

The second Waldorf-Astoria Hotel opened in its current location on Park Avenue in 1931.

Murray Hill

In the 19th century, the neighborhood was considered to be "uptown" with the City ending at Fifth Avenue and 42nd Street. Its boundaries are roughly from 28th to 40th Streets and from Madison to 3rd Avenue.

J.P. Morgan, an American financier, banker, and art collector built his mansion in the 1880s on Madison Avenue at 36th Street. Upon his death, he donated the property and his large book collection to the City as a public library and museum.

Opulent mansions were built between Fifth and Park Avenues and elegant brownstones between Park and Lexington Avenues. The stables and carriage houses that served the fine families stood between Lexington and Third Avenue.

Manhattan's wholesale Flower District was once home to major jazz musicians in the 1950s and '60s.

Throughout the 20th century, the neighborhood has become a quiet residential area.

The area on Lexington Avenue around 28th Street is informally now called "Curry Hill" due to the concentration of Indian restaurants and specialized grocery stores.

The Little Church Around the Corner

The Church of the Transfiguration, more often known as the Little Church Around the Corner, was founded in the 1840s. Set back behind an English garden, it is located on 29th Street.

For many years, "Murray Hill," or "MU," was used by the New York Telephone Company as a telephone exchange for residents living on the east side of Manhattan. Most neighborhoods at the time would be grouped together by a particular exchange name.

The Empire State Building

A 103-story landmark art deco skyscraper located at the intersection of Fifth Avenue and west 34th Street, its name is derived from the nickname for New York: the Empire State.

The building's original spire was designed to be a mooring mast and depot for airships. In 1953, a large broadcast tower was added to the top of the spire.

The Empire State Building has been named by the American Society of Civil Engineers as one of the Seven Wonders of the Modern World.

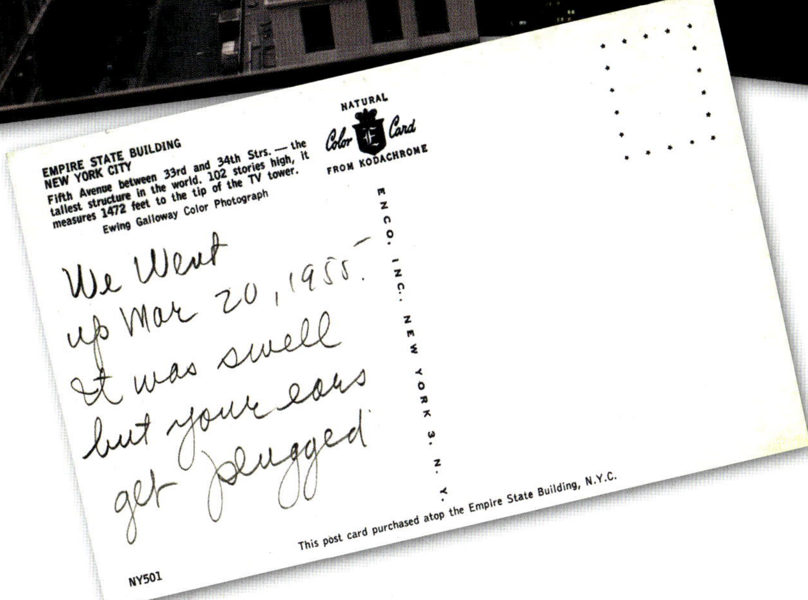

It stood as the world's tallest building for more than 40 years from its completion in 1930 until the construction of the Twin Towers in 1972.

Herald Square

One of the city's major newspapers, *The New York Herald* had its offices on the square.

The Hotel McAlpin, when it opened in 1912, was the largest hotel in the world. Most noted for the radio broadcasts that transmitted from the building, in the 1970s it was converted to rental apartments, and by 2001 to condominiums.

Across from Herald Square is Macy's flagship department store. For years, its archrival, Gimbels Brothers department store, was located in what is now the Manhattan Mall.

The Macy's Thanksgiving Day parade has set off the start of the holiday shopping season since 1924.

Woolworth's was one of America first five-and-dime stores. It originated the idea of the lunch counter to keep customers from leaving the store.

The Korean Business District has established itself between 5th and 6th Avenues, and 31st to 36th Streets.

Fifth Avenue & 42nd Street

In 1906, the department store B. Altman and Company occupied the whole block at 34th Street and Fifth Avenue. The result was the creation of a high-end shopping district that attracted fashionable women and other upscale stores. Lord and Taylor's flagship store is also located nearby on Fifth Avenue.

Fifth Avenue originates at Washington Square Park in Greenwich Village and runs northwards through the heart of Midtown and Harlem.

The Chrysler Building

Headquarters of the Chrysler Corporation was located at the intersection of 42nd Street and Lexington Avenue; from 1930 until the mid-1950s.

The Chrysler Building is considered a masterpiece of Art Deco architecture. The distinctive ornamentation of the building is based on features that were then being used on Chrysler automobiles.

It was the world's tallest building for 18 months before being surpassed by the Empire State Building in 1931.

Grand Central Terminal

Located at 42nd Street and Park Avenue, the grand Beaux-Arts style building opened in 1913, replacing an earlier station on the same site.

The new terminal combined multiple railroad lines into one station. The northbound tracks were buried underground, creating what is now Park Avenue.

The construction of Grand Central Terminal created a mini-city underground. It also spurred building throughout the neighborhood in the 1920s, including the Chrysler Building.

In the late 1960s plans were made to demolish the terminal in order to build a tower over the station. Thanks to the opposition from Jacqueline Kennedy Onassis and the New York City Landmarks Preservation Commission the original structure was preserved.

The News Building built in 1929 was the home of the *New York Daily News* until the mid-1990s. It is known as the model for the headquarters of the fictional newspaper *Daily Planet*, where Superman worked as journalist Clark Kent.

Turtle Bay

By the 20th century, the area of Turtle Bay was in decay, packed with breweries, gasworks, slaughter houses, coal yards, and railroad piers

Shanties lined the waterfront. The darkness cast from the 2nd and 3rd Avenue ELs, added with the numerous plants in the area, showered the district with the heaviest soot in the City.

The site of the United Nations Headquarters is located on Turtle Bay. The area extends between 41st and 53rd Streets, and eastward from Lexington Avenue to the East River.

The United Nations

Founded in 1945 after World War II to replace the League of Nations.

By the early 1950s, 18 acres were leveled for the construction of the UN Headquarters. High-rise office buildings and condominiums soon filled the neighborhood. The area is now known for its brownstones apartments, landscaped parks, tree-lined streets, and relatively quiet neighborhood atmosphere.

The UN is an international organization whose stated aims are facilitating cooperation in international law, international security, economic development, social progress, human rights, and achievement of world peace.

Tudor City & Sutton Place

In the 1920s, real estate developer Fred F. French sought to create Tudor City as an urban Utopia.

Sutton Place also became the address for fashionable socialites to build townhouses. With the view of the East River, grand co-operative apartment houses followed.

Development came to a halt with the Great Depression, and building in the area did not resume until the 1940s and '50s.

West Side

The New York Public Library

On the corner of Fifth Avenue and 42nd Street, it opened in 1911, and soon became the largest public library in North America.

Two famous stone lions guarding the entrance were originally named Leo Astor and Leo Lenox, in honor of the library's founders.

In the 1930s the lions were nicknamed "Patience" and "Fortitude" by Mayor Fiorello La Guardia. He chose these names because he felt that the citizens of New York would need to possess these qualities to see themselves through the Depression.

Bryant Park

In the early 1800s, the area was used as a potter's field and remained so until 1840, when thousands of bodies were moved to Wards Island. The first park opened in 1847 as Reservoir Square and was renamed Bryant Park when construction of the New York Library building began.

The construction of the Sixth Avenue elevated railway in 1878 cast a literal and metaphorical shadow over the park, and by the 1930s it had suffered from neglect and was considered disreputable.

The park was re-designed in 1933 as a Great Depression public works project under the leadership of Robert Moses. Its new features included a great lawn, hedges, trees, and later an iron fence to separate the park from the surrounding city street.

By the 1970s, Bryant Park was again disreputable, taken over by drug dealers, prostitutes, and the homeless.

From 1979 to 1983, the Parks Council brought back new life by developing a book and flower market, cafes, landscape improvements, and entertainment activities.

In 1994, Bryant Park became home to New York Fashion Week, held twice a year under large white tents.

Garment District

Since the early 20th century, the Garment District has been the center of fashion for New York's top designers, showrooms, wholesalers, sample production, and corporate offices.

Unable to travel to Paris during World War II, Americans turned to New York for the latest in fashion trends. Press Week started in the 1940s as a showcase of American talent and has turned into Fashion week.

POST CARD

NEW YORK N.Y. STA. M MAR 27 4-PM 1908

This side for Correspondence.

Send me my tan jacket at once. Getting a suit later. Got my summer hat. "Swell" Ethel

This side for Address.

Mrs. F. G. Chapm
Bristolville
Ohio
Trumbull Co.

The International Ladies' Garment Workers' Union was once one of the largest labor unions in the United States. It was a key player in the labor history of the 1920s and '30s.

Fueled by a skilled immigrant workforce, apparel manufacturing was once the largest industry in the City. By the 1980s, almost all manufacturing moved overseas.

The General Post Office

"Neither snow nor rain nor heat nor gloom of night stays these couriers from the swift completion of their appointed rounds."

Opened in 1912, as the City's main post office.

The grandeur of the Corinthian colonnade matched that of Pennsylvania Station, originally facing it across 8th Avenue. Designed by architects McKim, Mead and White, the building bears the famous inscription above.

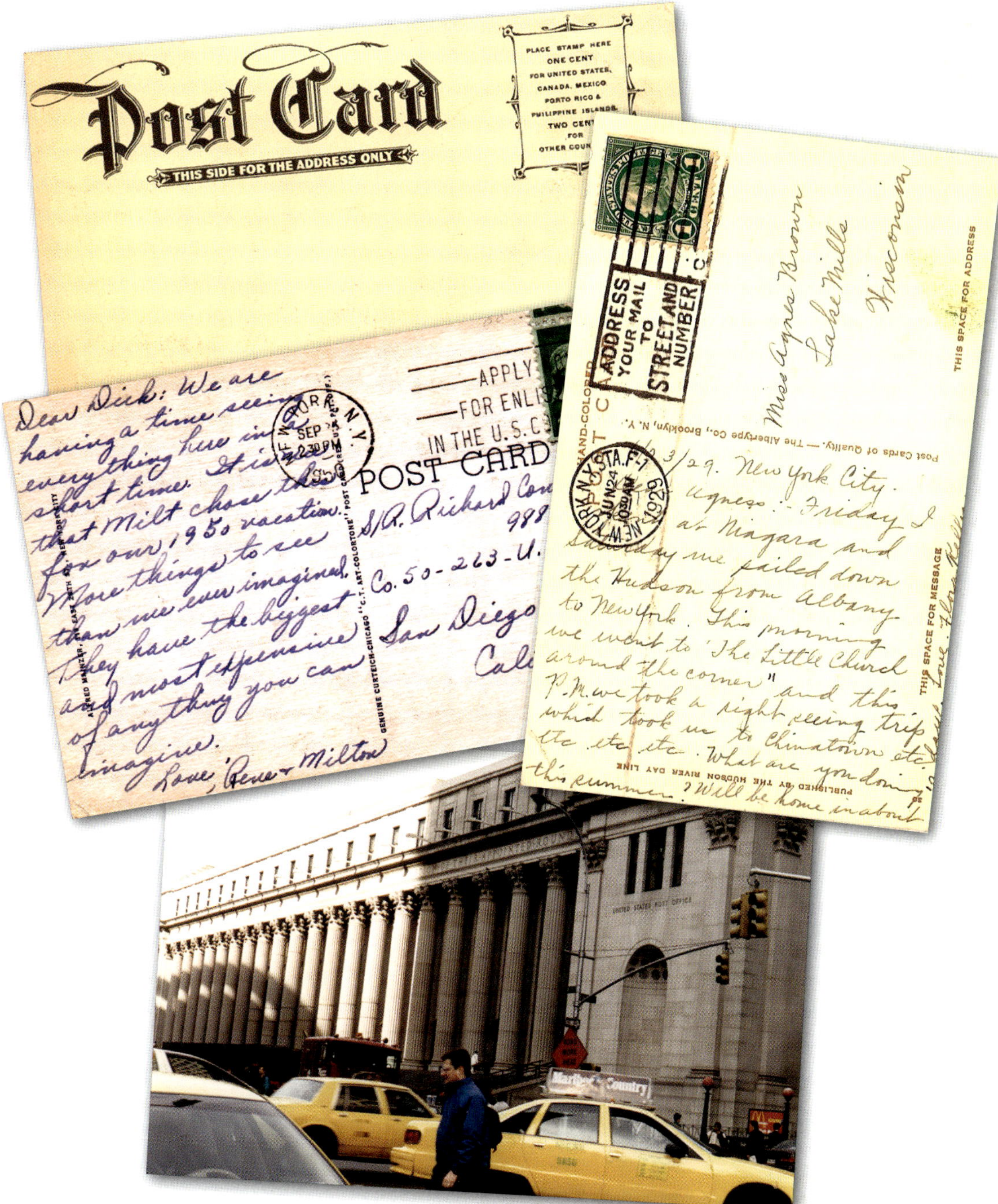

The Post Office was once open to the public 24 hours a day, 7 days a week.

In 1982, it was renamed the Farley Building to honor James A. Farley, the 53rd Postmaster General.

Pennsylvania Station

The original Beaux-Arts station was completed in 1910.
It was an architectural jewel of New York City.

The underground terminal allowed travelers to connect between
New Jersey, Manhattan, Long Island, and the Bronx.

It was demolished in 1963 to make way for the Pennsylvania Plaza
complex, including the fourth and current Madison Square Garden.

Public outcry over the demolished structure
led to the creation of the New York City
Landmarks Preservation Commission.

In 1968, the current Madison Square Garden was built above Pennsylvania Station. It was one of the first structures of its kind to be built above an active railroad system.

In the 1990s, the station was renovated with the original four-sided clock installed at the 34th Street Long Island Rail Road entrance. Artists were commissioned to create artwork to recall the grandeur of the old architecture. Penn Station is one of the busiest in the world, connecting suburban commuters with the City's underground subway system.

Clinton / Hell's Kitchen

A neighborhood between 34th and 59th Street, from 8th Avenue to the Hudson River. In the mid-19th century, poor Irish immigrants settled in shantytowns along the Hudson River. Many of these immigrants found work on the docks nearby or along the railroads that carried freight along 11th Avenue.

During prohibition in the 1920s, many of the warehouses operated as breweries, escalating violence in the community.

In the 1950s, Italian and Puerto Rican immigrants moved into the area. Gang wars gave the neighborhood the reputation of "Hell's Kitchen." The name stuck and the stigma kept housing prices low. With its proximity to Broadway theaters and the Actors Studio, the neighborhood is a haven for aspiring actors and musicians.

Port Authority Bus Terminal

Beginning operations in 1950, it originally occupied only the block between 40th and 41st Streets between 8th and 9th Avenue.

The 1970s and '80s brought expansion and revitalization. The Art Deco styling of the original terminal has been replaced with a modern steel-and-glass facade.

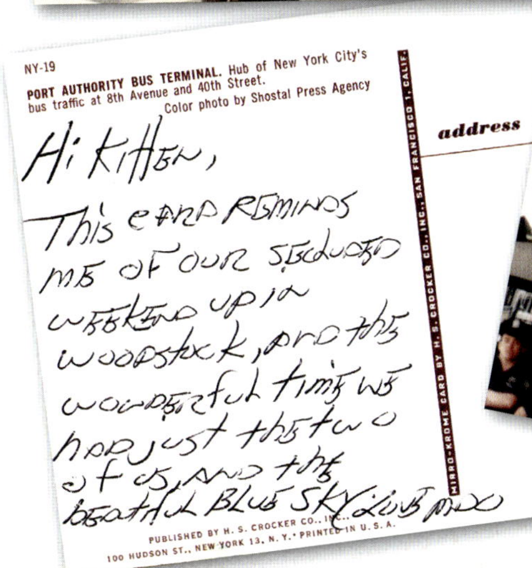

Times Square & 42nd Street

Times Square is at the junction of Broadway and 7th Avenue and stretches from west 42nd to west 47th Street.

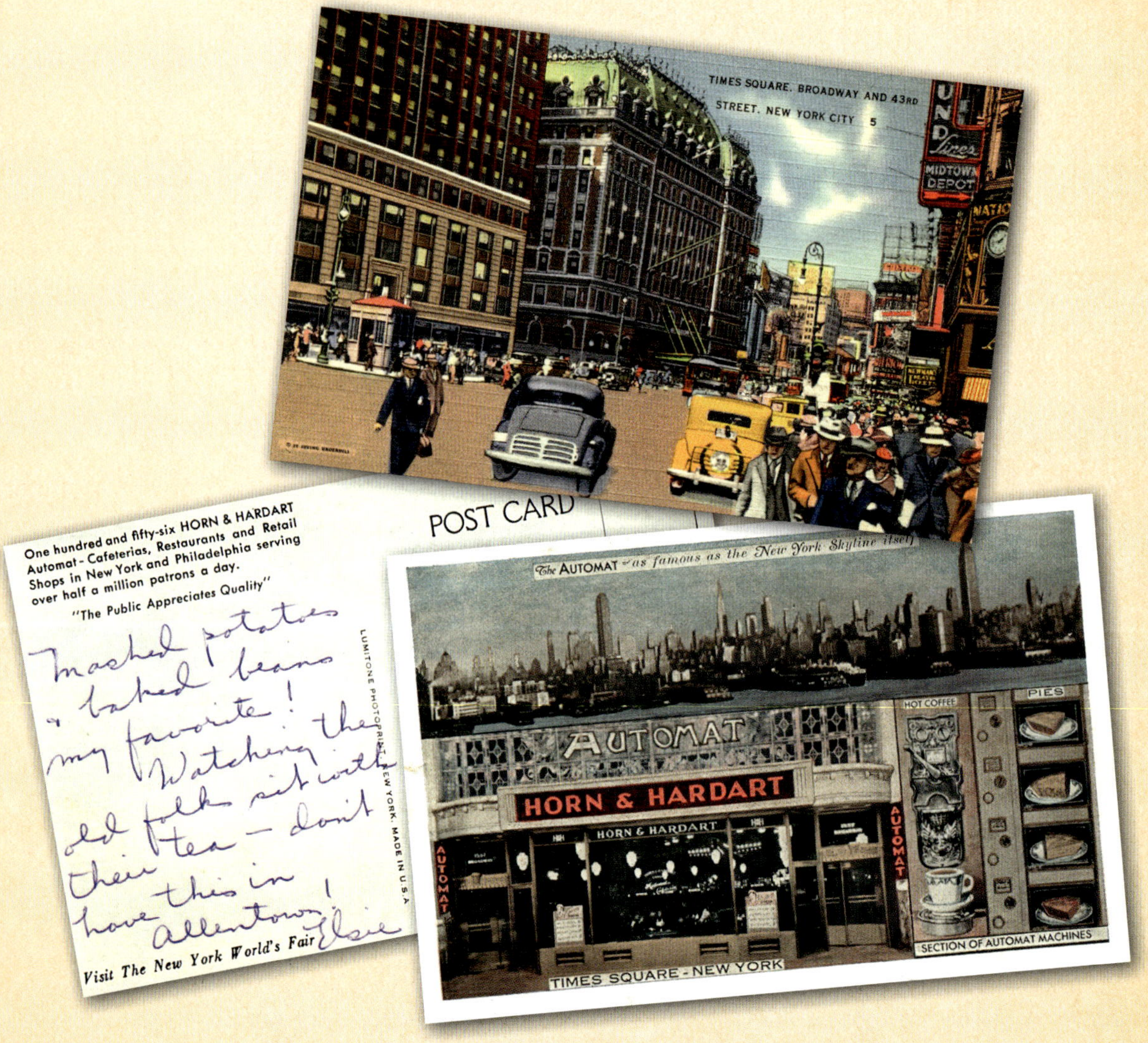

The Horn & Hardart's Automat opened on Times Square in 1912. Reflecting the attitude of the industrial revolution, it was one of the first restaurants to introduce coin-operated vending machines instead of waitresses.

Knickerbocker Hotel

Built in 1903 by John Jacob Astor IV and located on the corner of Broadway and 42nd Street, the hotel was a showcase of luxury in a time of economic prosperity.

One of the legends connected with the hotel comes from the drink called the martini, which was said to have been invented by the house bartender, Martini di Arma di Tagga. In 1912, he mixed dry vermouth and gin together and the mixture gained the favor of John D. Rockefeller, who liked it so much that he recommended it to all his Wall Street buddies.

The "Knickerbocker" subway sign is posted over a doorway that once connected to the hotel as a private rail line for Astor and his privileged guests. The train, which connected Times Square with Grand Central Station, is now used as the 42nd Street shuttle.

The hotel was later turned into offices and was the home of *Newsweek* magazine and garment showrooms. Plans are to return it to a luxury hotel.

Times Square

Formerly named Longacre Square, Times Square was renamed in 1904 after the *New York Times* moved its headquarters to the newly erected Times Building.

Times Square, nicknamed "The Crossroads of the World," has achieved the status of an iconic world landmark. It is a symbol of the energy of New York City.

The *New York Times* moved to more spacious offices across Broadway in 1913. The old Times Building is known as One Times Square. The site is famous for the annual New Year's Eve ball drop where over a million people come every year to celebrate.

The "Big Apple" is a nickname for New York City that has been around since the 1920s.

Broadway

The Theatre District extends from 40th to 54th Street; from 6th to 8th Avenue, and includes Times Square.

Theaters did not arrive in the area until the early 1900s.

Florenz Ziegfeld produced annual spectacular song-and-dance revues on Broadway, featuring extravagant sets and elaborate costumes. The "Ziegfeld Follies" (1907 to 1931) were based on the Parisian "Folies Bergere."

The Shubert Brothers were theatrical producers of the largest theater empire in the 20th century.

The introduction of motion pictures created a challenge to the stage. At first, films were silent and presented only limited competition.

The musical films of the "Roaring Twenties" emphasized big dance routines and popular songs of the day. *The Jazz Singer* showcased synchronized sound and critics wondered if the cinema would replace live theatre altogether.

42nd Street

In the 1930s, the Great Depression led to a decline in theater attendance, forcing many businesses to close.

For decades, 42nd Street acquired a reputation as an undesirable area. By the 1960s, it became a haven for adult XXX entertainment, striptease, peep shows, drug dealers, and prostitutes. By the mid-'70s, Times Square was dangerous and avoided by tourists.

In the 1990s, Walt Disney Company announced it would invest in revitalizing the street, staging theatrical productions.

The so-called "Disneyfication" has turned the community into a family-friendly destination, bringing in billions in tourist revenue.

Neon Jungle

In 1917, the first large electric billboard was installed. The bright lights attracted tourists to the area. Zoning now requires that all buildings must be illuminated with signs.

Officially, signs in Times Square are called "spectaculars," and the largest of them are called "jumbotrons." The bright lights of Times Square rival that of Las Vegas.

Rockefeller Center

Named after John D. Rockefeller, Jr., who leased the space from Columbia University. He initially planned to build an opera house for the Metropolitan Opera on the site. After the stock market crash of 1929, the plans changed.

Rockefeller Plaza

In its time, Rockefeller Center was the largest private building project ever undertaken. Construction of the 14 Art Deco buildings began in 1930 and was completed in 1939.

Air view of the 70-story R.C.A. Building and the 38-story International Building, Rockefeller Center. The R.C.A. building has over 63 acres of floor space, one of its tenants being the N.B.C. with 28 studios. On the 11th floor is Horticultural Hall, and at this level over the N.B.C. is the Garden of the Nations with two thousand trees and twenty thousand flowering bulbs. The 2-story Rainbow Room for dining and dancing occupies the 65th floor, and the Observation Roof 850 feet above New York is the mecca for sightseers. The International Building, 520 feet high, has a 4-story lobby of dark green marble and a copper leaf ceiling. World expositions fade into shadows before these giant palaces that cannot be described.

POST CARD

GRAND CENT ANNEX N.Y. OCT 4 PM 1931

BUY U.S. SAVINGS BONDS ASK YOUR

LUMITONE PHOTOPRINT, NEW YORK. MADE IN U.S.A.

Dear Eliz: We are having one thrill in N.Y. and seeing + doing all we can possible. got in Heard + met Maj. Bowes Thurs. Eve. We are seeing all the Broadway hits. Geo. is at the Medical Center and I am doing 5th Ave. It is exciting - so different from any other place. We came by train. Love. Lucile.

Miss Elizabeth Klemer
1710 Lee St.
Commerce
Texas.

In the summer, the sunken plaza becomes an outdoor restaurant; in the winter, an ice skating rink.

The tradition of a Christmas tree at Rockefeller Center began in 1931, when construction workers decorated a small balsam fir tree with garlands of cranberries, paper, and tin cans.

Radio City Music Hall

Opened to the public in 1932, the music hall became the premiere showcase for spectacular stage shows and films from RKO Radio Studio.

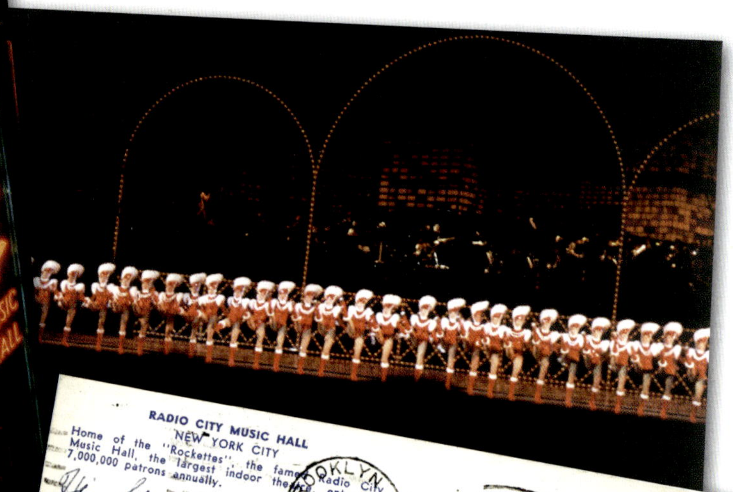

In the late 1970s, plans were made to convert the theater into office space. Instead, the landmark theater was renovated and reopened to the public.

NBC Television Studios

Broadcasts from 30 Rockefeller Plaza across the street from Radio City Music Hall.

The McGraw-Hill Building

One of three steel and glass skyscrapers developed between McGraw-Hill Publishing and Rockefeller Center, erected in the 1970s.

Saint Patrick's Cathedral

The famous Cathedral is located on the east side of Fifth Avenue between 50th and 51st Street, and was completed in 1878.

The Easter Parade along Fifth Avenue became an annual tradition of displaying extravagant fashion and outrageous hats. Fifth Avenue is also the route for many parades including the St. Patrick's Day.

Fifth Avenue

By the turn of the 20th century, wealthy New Yorkers had migrated uptown to build their mansions. The stretch of Fifth Avenue between 59th and 96th Streets facing Central Park became prime real estate.

The bronze statue across the street from St. Patrick's Cathedral depicts the ancient Greek Titan Atlas holding the heavens. The Art Deco statue stands in front of Rockefeller Plaza as a symbol of power and strength.

Fifth Avenue between 49th and 60th Streets is lined with prestigious shops, consistently ranked as one of the most expensive streets in the world.

Carnegie Hall

Built by philanthropist Andrew Carnegie in 1891, it is one of the most prestigious concert venues located east of 7th Avenue between 56th and 57th Streets.

Fifth Avenue serves as the dividing line for building numbering in Manhattan, separating the east side from the west side.

Central Park

59th Street & Central Park South

Central Park South is on 59th Street and it forms the southern perimeter of Central Park. It is bounded by Columbus Circle at 8th Avenue on the west and Grand Army Plaza at Fifth Avenue to the east. With entrances to the park at Artist Gate at 6th, Artisans Gate at $7^{th,}$ and Merchants Gate at 8th Avenue.

Central Park South is famous for upscale hotels like the Plaza, Ritz-Carlton, Park Lane, and Essex House; each offering magnificent views of Central Park. The street is located just steps away from Fifth and Madison Avenue shopping and Carnegie Hall.

The Plaza Hotel

A landmark 20-story luxury hotel on the west side of Grand Army Plaza, from which it derives its name. When it first opened in 1907, a room for a night cost $2.50.

59TH STREET
NEW YORK CITY
CENTRAL PARK SOUTH . . . the street with the world's most renowned and elite hotels. In the background can be seen the famous Coliseum and the Hudson River.
H-440
address
CENTRAL PARK
NEW YORK CITY

In the 1850s a horse-drawn carriage was the only way to travel in the park. Today, horse-drawn carriages line up on 59th Street and are a popular tourist attraction for a ride through the park. At night the horses return to Hell's Kitchen to stay in stables just off the Westside Highway.

Columbus Circle

The coordinates of Columbus Circle form the point from which all longitude and latitude from New York City are measured.

It is located at the intersection of Broadway, Central Park West, Central Park South (59th Street), and 8th Avenue.

Columbus Circle, named for the explorer Christopher Columbus, was completed in 1905 and renovated a century later.

The area was also revitalized when the Time Warner Center was constructed to include the broadcast studios of CNN, a luxury hotel, shops, restaurants, and a concert hall.

Central Park

Designed by landscape designer Frederick Law Olmsted and the English architect Calvert Vaux in 1858 after winning a competition. They also designed Brooklyn's Prospect Park.

While the park appears natural, it is in fact almost entirely man-made. The park contains several lakes and ponds that have been created artificially.

The park at one time included bridle paths, two ice-skating rinks, a conservatory garden, a wildlife sanctuary, and a large area of natural woods. It also has a 106-acre reservoir, a zoo, a castle, and a place to rent rowboats and ride a Victorian carousel.

Central Park stretches over 840 acres, from 59th to 110th Street and from Fifth Avenue to Central Park West (8th Avenue).

From the 1860s until 1934, Sheep Meadow actually held grazing sheep. During the Depression they were moved upstate, as it was feared they might be stolen for food.

On weekends and in the evenings, when cars are banned, the 6 miles of drives within the park are used by joggers, bicyclists and skaters.

The park is an oasis in the middle of a busy city. There are fields for team sports, quiet areas, and lots of playgrounds and events for all.

In the 1960s, the great lawn became a venue for events of unprecedented scale, including political rallies, demonstrations, festivals, and massive concerts.

Upper East Side

The Queensboro Bridge & Tram

The bridge was completed in 1909 and designated as a national landmark in 1973. It is a double cantilever bridge, spanning the East River and connecting Long Island City, in the borough of Queens, with Manhattan. The 59th Street Bridge is also known as the Ed Koch Queensboro Bridge.

Trolleys to and from Queens stopped in the middle of the bridge to meet an elevator down, which was the only access to Roosevelt Island. They remained in service until the late 1950s long after most trolley service had been dismantled.

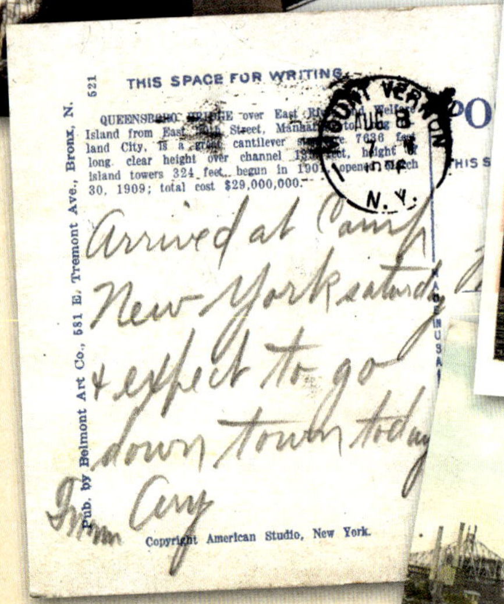

In 2000, the north outer roadway of the bridge was converted into a pedestrian walk and bicycle path.

The Roosevelt Island Tramway

Constructed in the 1970s to connect Roosevelt Island directly with Manhattan.

Originally intended as a temporary measure,
it is now a permanent attraction.

The tram runs above the East River on the north side of the Queensboro Bridge providing breathtaking views of Manhattan.

Roosevelt Island

Known as Welfare Island from the 1920s to 1973. The narrow island in the East River runs from Manhattan's 46th to 85th Streets, and once housed a lunatic asylum, hospital, and a prison.

The Welfare Island Bridge from Queens opened in the 1950s, allowing cars and trucks onto the island.

By the 1970s, Roosevelt Island was redeveloped to accommodate low-to-mid income housing projects. In 1989, subway service to the island began, 13 years after originally scheduled. Today Roosevelt Island offers spectacular views of the city from luxury condominiums.

FDR Drive

Originally named the East River Drive, the roadway was later renamed after President Franklin Delano Roosevelt. The FDR Drive starts at Battery Park and goes north to 125th Street, where it becomes the Harlem River Drive.

Upper East Side

Yorkville

The boundaries of Yorkville roughly include the East River to Lexington Avenue and 72nd to 96th Street. For much of the 19th and 20th centuries, the area was a working-class neighborhood.

The neighborhood was the ultimate melting pot; its western half was referred to as "Irishtown." The Bohemians—Czech, Polish, and Slovak peoples—lived there from 65th to 73rd Streets.

"Little Hungary," a hub for the Austro-Hungarian immigrants, was from 75th to 83rd Street.

Lenox Hill Hospital, formally the German Hospital, was renamed as a result of anti-German sentiment during World War I.

The Ruppert family operated one of the largest breweries in Manhattan and in 1913 employed over 1,000 men. For 24 years, Jacob Ruppert owned the NY Yankees and built the team into a baseball powerhouse.

Located from 2nd to 3rd Avenue between 90th and 93rd Street, the site today houses the Ruppert Yorkville Towers.

Second Avenue EL

The Second Avenue elevated trains ran from City Hall to 129th Street until 1942. The Third Avenue elevated line operated a block to the west and was demolished in 1956.

Currently, the Upper East Side is served by the IRT Lexington Avenue line. As a result, East Yorkville became slightly isolated, allowing it to remain a more affordable neighborhood in walking distance to Central Park.

The need for a subway line under Manhattan's 2nd Avenue was realized shortly after the First World War. Work on the line never commenced, as the Great Depression crushed all financing. In recent years, as the East Side of Manhattan has experienced significant residential development, the demand for another subway line has become necessary.

The 2nd Avenue Subway project plans to ultimately connect Harlem south to the Financial District.

Gracie Mansion

The official residence of the Mayor of the City of New York. The mansion, built in the 1790s, overlooks the East River. It is located in Carl Schurz Park, at East End Avenue and 88th Streets.

Park Avenue

The thoroughfare was originally known as 4th Avenue and carried the tracks of the New York and Harlem railroads. When the Grand Central Depot was opened in the 1870s, the railroad tracks between 56th and 96th Streets were sunk below street level. In 1888, Park Avenue was extended to the Harlem River.

In the 1920s the portion of Park Avenue from Grand Central Terminal to 96th Street saw extensive construction of luxury apartments.

The MetLife Building (formerly Pan Am Building) was the largest commercial office building in the world when it opened in 1963.

Park Avenue is a wide boulevard that allows for north and southbound traffic. The medians are planted with flowers and trees throughout the year. A Park Avenue address is considered to be one of the most expensive in the world.

Museum Mile

A section of Fifth Avenue running from 82nd to 110th Street on the Upper East Side is the area known as Carnegie Hill. The architecture here included mansions, apartment buildings, brownstones, townhouses, and some of New York's most famous museums.

Many of New York's elite established residence along Fifth Avenue with breathtaking views of Central Park.

The Guggenheim Museum

Designed by Frank Lloyd Wright, it opened in 1959 to much controversy for its sharp contrast to the surrounding buildings. Today it is considered to be one of the 20th century's most important architectural landmarks.

The Metropolitan Museum of Art

The "MET" looks over Central Park at 82nd Street. It was founded in the 1870s to bring art and art education to the American people.

The Museum Mile Festival was established in the 1970s to increase public awareness of the arts.

Some of the museums that take part in the event include the Cooper-Hewitt, Frick Collection, Museum of African Art, El Museo del Barrio, the Jewish Museum and the Museum of the City of New York.

Upper West Side

The neighborhood that lies between Central Park and the Hudson River from 59th to 125th Street.

In the early 1900s, the area south of 67th Street was heavily populated by African-Americans. It was sometimes referred to as "San Juan Hill" in commemoration of the African-American soldiers for their role in the Spanish-American War.

For quite some time it was a neighborhood of tenement housing and rival gangs.

By the 1960s, the area was cleared to make room for the Lincoln Park complex.

Demolition was delayed to allow for filming the exterior shots of the movie *West Side Story.*

Lincoln Center for the Performing Arts

The Lincoln Center complex centralized major cultural institutions into one location and was the first of its kind in America.

John D. Rockefeller III is credited with raising more than half of the $184,000,000 in private funds needed to build the center.

Over the next 30 years the previously blighted area around Lincoln Center became a new cultural hub for performing arts.

The Upper West Side bordering Central Park is now an upscale residential area.

The Dakota Apartment Building

Constructed in the late 1800s. At that time the Upper West Side of Manhattan was sparsely inhabited and considered to be as remote as the Dakota Territory. Across the street in Central Park is Strawberry Fields, a memorial to musician John Lennon; who was murdered outside the building in 1980.

The American Museum of Natural History

Founded in 1869, it is located at 79th Street across from Central Park. The Museum has a full-time scientific staff, research laboratories, renowned library, and sponsors special field expeditions each year. Its exhibitions attract about five million visitors annually.

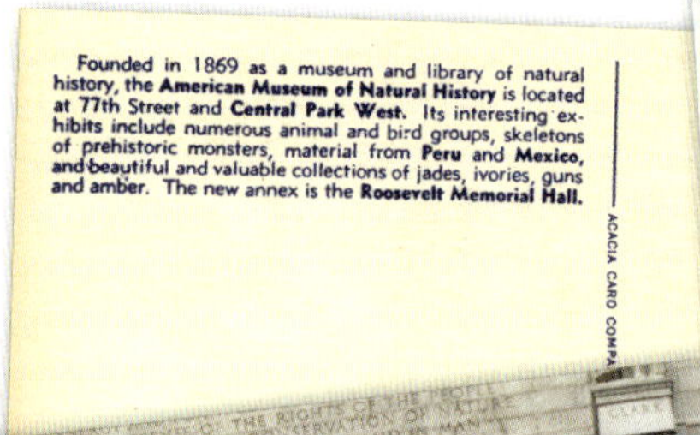

Founded in 1869 as a museum and library of natural history, the **American Museum of Natural History** is located at 77th Street and **Central Park West.** Its interesting exhibits include numerous animal and bird groups, skeletons of prehistoric monsters, material from **Peru** and **Mexico,** and beautiful and valuable collections of jades, ivories, guns and amber. The new annex is the **Roosevelt Memorial Hall.**

ACACIA CARD COMPA

This Upper West Side park surrounding the American Museum of Natural History is named to honor Theodore Roosevelt, the 26th President.

Hayden Planetarium

Built on 81st Street in 1935, it is one of the main attractions of the Rose Center for Earth and Space. Its mission: to bring the frontier of astrophysics to the public.

The West Side Highway

The West Side Highway runs south from 72nd Street along the Hudson River to the southern tip of Manhattan. North of 72nd Street, it is properly known as the Henry Hudson Parkway.

Construction of the West Side elevated highway started in 1929 and was completed in 1951. The highway was obsolete almost from the beginning. Its lanes were considered too narrow for trucks and its exit ramps were hazardous.

In 1973, a portion of the elevated highway collapsed under the weight of a dump truck, which was carrying asphalt for ongoing road repairs.

Through the '70s and '80s, controversial rebuilding proposals included burying the highway south of 40th Street (called the Westway Project). The original elevated highway was dismantled in 1989; traffic was rerouted to temporary highways and the project was finally completed in 2001.

The West Side Piers

The New York Passenger Ship Terminals were first completed in 1935. The terminals were built to handle the big luxury liners that had outgrown the docks at Chelsea Piers.

Renovated in the 1970s, Piers 88, 90 and 92 are on the Hudson River between 46th and 54th Street. These piers are the site of many events all year around, including the world famous New York Flower Show.

Amsterdam Avenue

In 1890, 10th Avenue was renamed Amsterdam Avenue. Real estate developers felt the new name would make the area more popular; and that the section of Manhattan could become "the new city" and a "new, New Amsterdam."

The name Bloomingdale is still used in reference to a part of the Upper West Side, essentially the location of old Bloomingdale Village. The area runs from about 96th to 110th Street, and from Riverside Park east to Amsterdam Avenue.

Riverside Park

Completed in 1910, it consisted of a narrow strip of land between the Hudson River and Riverside Drive.

The scenic waterfront park was designed to create the appearance of a natural extension to the Hudson River Valley.

When the park was first laid out, access to the river was blocked by the New York Central Railroad.

In 1937, Robert Moses completed the "Westside Improvement Project," which added 132 acres of land to the park. It created a promenade by covering the tracks of the railroad, and made way for the development of the Henry Hudson Parkway.

Grant's Tomb

Grant's Tomb was built in 1897 for Ulysses S. Grant, situated in a prominent location overlooking the Hudson River. By the 1970s, it had become badly vandalized and covered in graffiti. After much public outcry, the tomb was restored and rededicated in the 1990s.

Riverside South

Since the 1960s plans have been in development to expand Riverside Park south of 59th Street, incorporating the former Penn Central freight rail yards.

In the 1990s, real estate developer Donald Trump in cooperation with civic partners began construction on one of the largest residential development transactions in New York City's history. The neighborhood will include more than 10,000 new homes, retail stores, and restaurants, and will add an additional 27 acres of waterfront park.

Columbia University

Founded and chartered as King's College in 1754, it is the oldest institution of higher education in the State of New York.

King's College became Columbia College after the American Revolution. In 1896 it was further renamed Columbia University.

The elevated IRT Ninth Avenue line was built in the 1800s and demolished in the 1940s.

At 110th Street it was known as "suicide curve."

Morningside Heights

This community is bounded by Morningside Park to the east, Riverside Park to the west, and 110th Street north to Harlem.

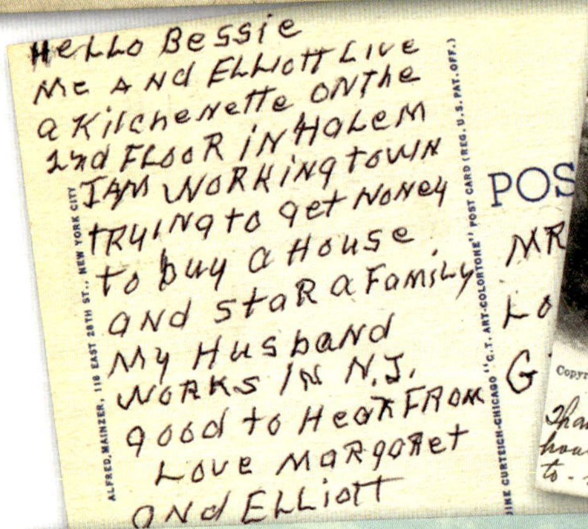

Some residents consider the area to be part of Upper West Side, while others call it part of Harlem. Because of its many universities, the neighborhood is also referred to as "college town."

The Cathedral of St. John the Divine

Designed in the late 1800s, it has undergone radical stylistic changes through the years.

It was originally designed to be Byzantine/Romanesque, the plan was changed after 1909 to reflect a Gothic style.

The cathedral is known for its major musical events including the celebration of the feast day of St. Francis of Assisi and the blessing of the animals.

Harlem

Harlem was given its name by the Dutch after the city of Haarlem in the Netherlands.

In the early 1900s, a great migration of former southern slaves arrived in New York and made Harlem their home.

The "Harlem Renaissance" in the '20s and '30s turned the community into a center for African-American business and gave birth to a cultural revolution.

The Savoy Ballroom

A renowned venue on Lenox Avenue for swing dancing and jazz, immortalized in the popular song "Stompin' at the Savoy." The ballroom was one of the first integrated dance halls where white and black Americans could dance together.

The Apollo Theater

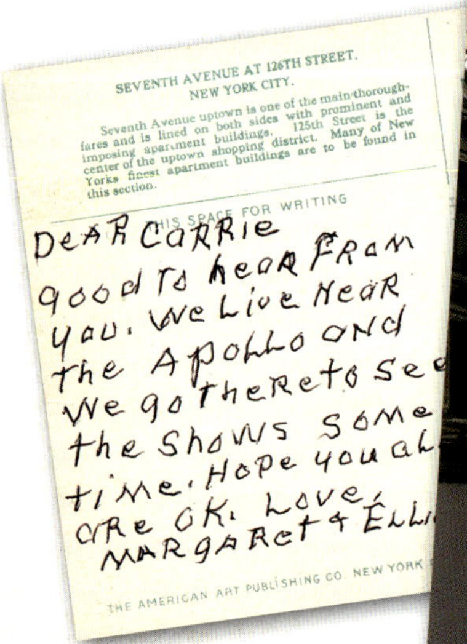

Opened in 1914 on W. 125th Street, in a former burlesque house, and remains today as one of the most famous African-American music halls.

It is home of *Showtime at the Apollo*, a nationally syndicated televised talent show that launched the careers of Billie Holiday, Ella Fitzgerald, Sarah Vaughan, and the Jackson Five.

The effects of the Great Depression devastated the community of Harlem. The City's loss of industry after World War II further plummeted employment opportunities. Poverty and crime increased.

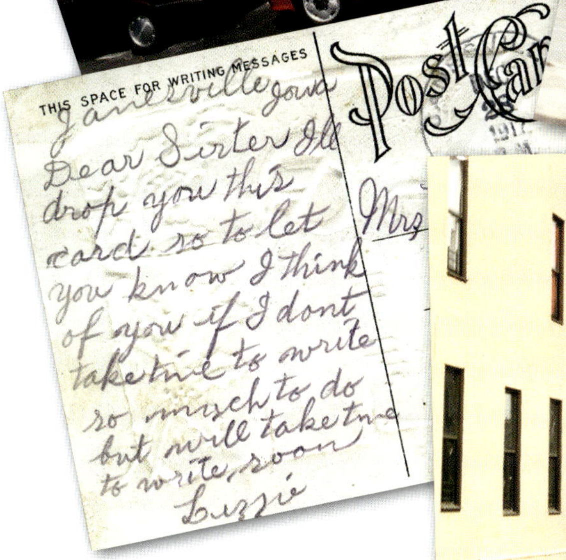

Harlem became Manhattan's most desperate neighborhood in the 1970s and early '80s when the city government, in lieu of tax payments, took ownership of more than half of Harlem's real estate.

By the mid-1990s, Harlem was considered by young professionals to be an up and coming neighborhood; and by the 21st century, it experienced social and economic gentrification.

The community of Harlem is currently experiencing a building boom and a new Renaissance.

Spanish Harlem

East Harlem's boundaries stretch from 96th Street to the Harlem River and from the East River to Fifth Avenue.

In the late 19th and early 20th century the area was home to immigrants from southern Italy and known as Italian Harlem.

In the 1950s, the area became one of the largest Latino communities in the City and has since been renamed Spanish Harlem

Uptown North

The Triboro Bridge

A complex of three separate bridges spanning the Harlem River, the Bronx Kill, and Hell Gate (part of the East River), the bridges connect the boroughs of Manhattan, Queens, and the Bronx via Randall's Island and Wards Island (which are joined by landfill).

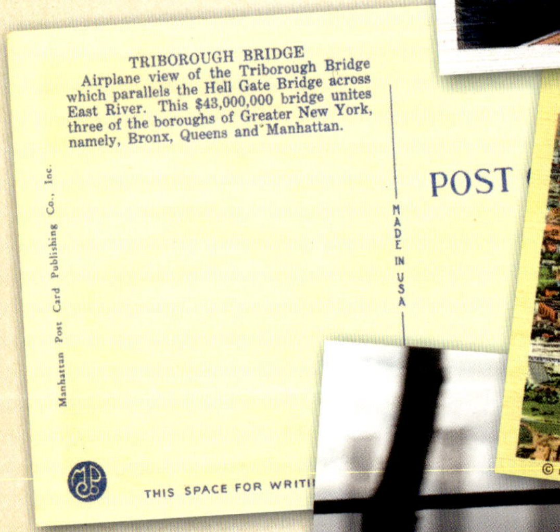

Hell Gate is a narrow tidal strait in the East River that gained its name for the area's numerous shipwrecks. It is still considered difficult to navigate due to strong tidal flows from the Long Island Sound, Harlem River strait, and the Upper Bay of New York Harbor.

Construction on the Triboro Bridge began on Black Friday in 1929.
Financing for the Triboro project came to a halt.

Using New Deal money, building resumed in the early 1930s and the bridge was opened to traffic in 1936.

Toll revenues from the bridge subsidize the New York City Transit Authority and the commuter railroads.

In 2008, the bridge was renamed the RFK Bridge, in memory of Robert F. Kennedy.

The Harlem River

A navigable tidal strait that flows 8 miles between the Hudson and the East River, separating the boroughs of Manhattan and the Bronx.

The Harlem River is spanned by seven swing bridges; three lift bridges and four arch bridges.

The Harlem River Drive runs along the banks of the river on the Manhattan side.

Manhattan Waterfront Greenway

The project connects a pathway for walking or cycling, 32 miles long, around the island of Manhattan. There are 3 principal greenways operated by the NYC Department of Parks.

The Harlem River Greenway, also known as Harlem River Speedway, is the shortest and completely uninterrupted. Beginning at the north end of Central Harlem, it runs to Dyckman Street in northern Manhattan.

The Hudson River Greenway is the longest, running along the West Side, from Dyckman Street in the north to Battery Park in the south, mostly through Riverside Park and Hudson River Park.

The East River Greenway runs from the Battery, past South Street Seaport to East Harlem with a 1.3-mile gap from 34th to 60th Streets. Here pedestrians must use 1st and 2nd Avenues to get around the United Nations complex.

The George Washington Bridge

A suspension bridge spanning the Hudson River, it connects the Washington Heights neighborhood of Manhattan to Fort Lee in New Jersey.

The bridge first opened in 1931 and included 6 lanes for traffic. In 1946, 2 additional lanes were added. A second, lower deck, which had been anticipated in the original plans, opened in 1962.

GEORGE WASHINGTON BRIDGE

Spans the Hudson River between Fort Lee, N. J. and New York City. One of the longest suspension bridges in the world. 4,760 feet long between the two 600 foot towers. Enough wire in the cables to go around the world four times. 131 illuminated directional signs to help guide your travel. Two levels and 14 traffic lanes are capable of handling almost 200,000 cars, trucks and buses per average day.

PLACE STAMP

Manhattan Post Card Pub. Co., Inc., 913 Broadway, N.Y.C., N.Y.

dp MADE BY DEXTER PRESS, INC. WEST NYACK, NEW YORK

70333-B

The original design for the towers called for them to be encased in concrete and granite. To cut costs, this was never done. The exposed crisscrossed steel towers have become one of the bridge's most distinctive design characteristics.

A few blocks north of the bridge is Bennet Park, built on the site of Fort Washington, a Revolutionary stronghold. The location marks the highest point on Manhattan Island overlooking the Hudson River.

Dyckman Street takes its name from the Dyckman farmhouse built in 1784, and is the oldest remaining farmhouse in Manhattan.

Washington Heights stretches from the Hudson River to Harlem River from 155th Street to Dyckman Street. The northwestern portion of Dyckman Street separates Inwood Hill Park and Fort Tryon Park.

The Cloisters

A branch of the Metropolitan Museum of Art, it is located in Fort Tryon Park. The Cloisters is a reconstructed medieval abbey, which sits atop the northern tip of Manhattan Island, overlooking the Hudson River.

The original architectural elements came from several European medieval abbeys, which were brought to the United States in pieces and reconstructed in the 1930s.

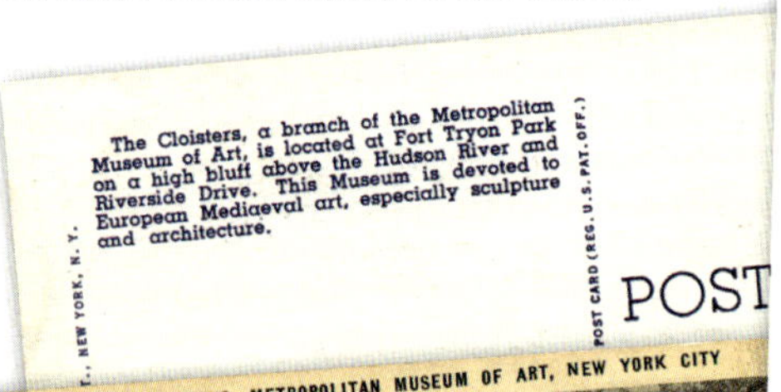

The museum and adjacent park was created through an endowment by philanthropist John D. Rockefeller, Jr.

Rockefeller bequeathed the majority of his medieval art collection to the Metropolitan Museum of Art. He also purchased several hundred acres of the Palisades directly across the river and donated it to the State of New Jersey. His foresight forever preserved the natural view from the Cloisters of the Hudson River.

Bibliography

Berman, John. *Ellis Island.* (New York: Barnes & Noble, 2003).

Kennedy, Rod. *Lost New York in Old Postcards.* (Layton, Utah: Gibbs Smith, 2001).

Kieran, John. *A Natural History of New York City.* (New York: Fordham University Press, 1982).

Kobayashi, Yumiko & Ryo Watanabe. *New York Detail.* (San Francisco, CA: Chronicle Books, 1995).

Patterson, Jerry E. *The City of New York New York.* (New York: Harry N. Abrams, Inc., 1978).

Silver, Nathan. *Lost New York, New York.* (New York: American Legacy Press, 1967).

Stookey, Lee. *Subway Ceramics: a History and Iconography.* (New York: Lee Stookey, 1992).

Tauranac, John & Christopher Little. *Elegant New York.* (New York: Cross River Press, Ltd., 1985).

Valentine, D.T. *Manual of the Corporation of the City of New York 1866.* (New York: Edmund Jones & Co., 1866).

Watson, Edward & Edmund Gillion, Jr., *New York: Then and Now.* (New York: Dover Press, 1976).

Wolfe, Gerard R. *New York: A Guide to the Metropolis Walking Tours of Architecture and History.* (New York: New York University Press, 1975).

Map of Manhattan

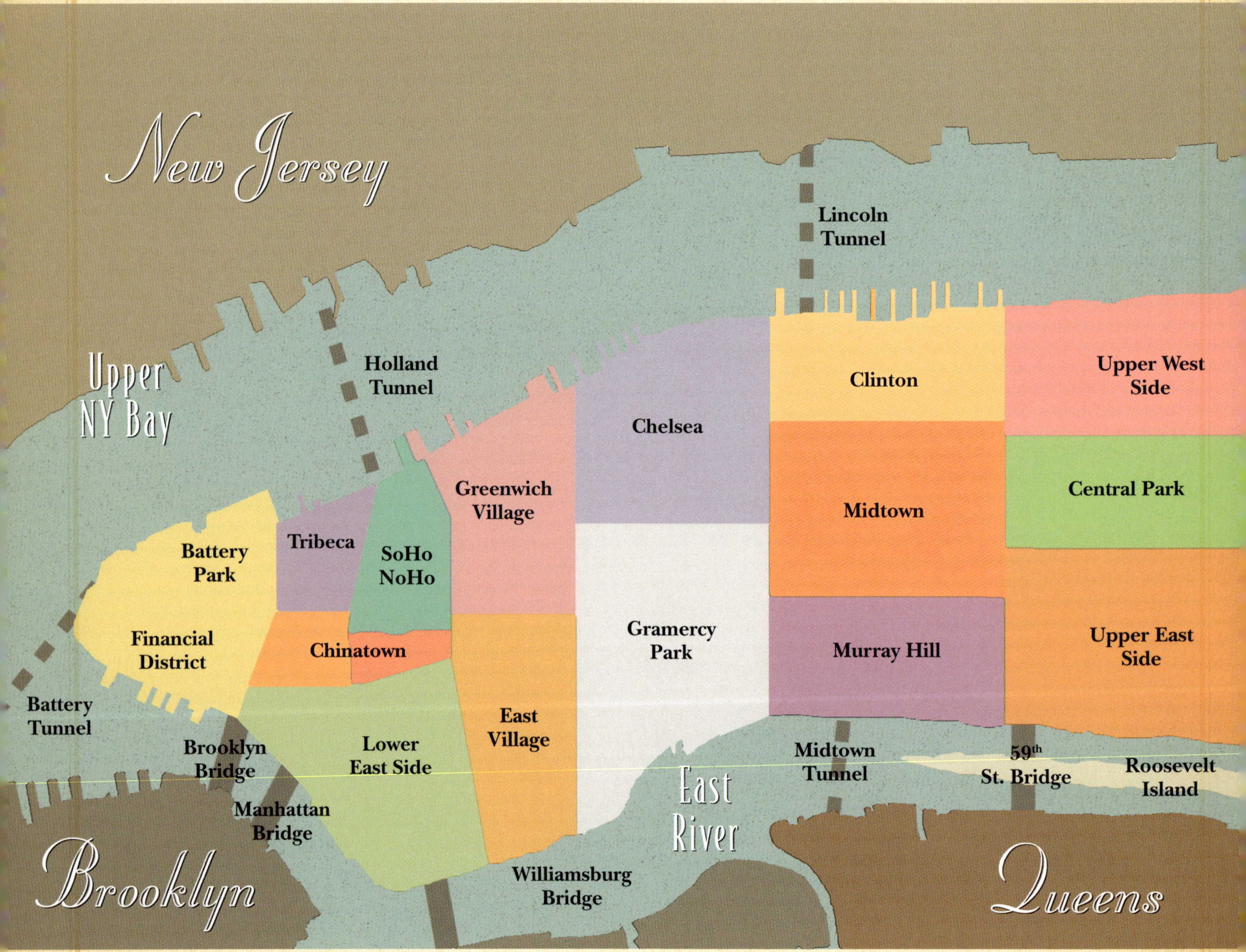

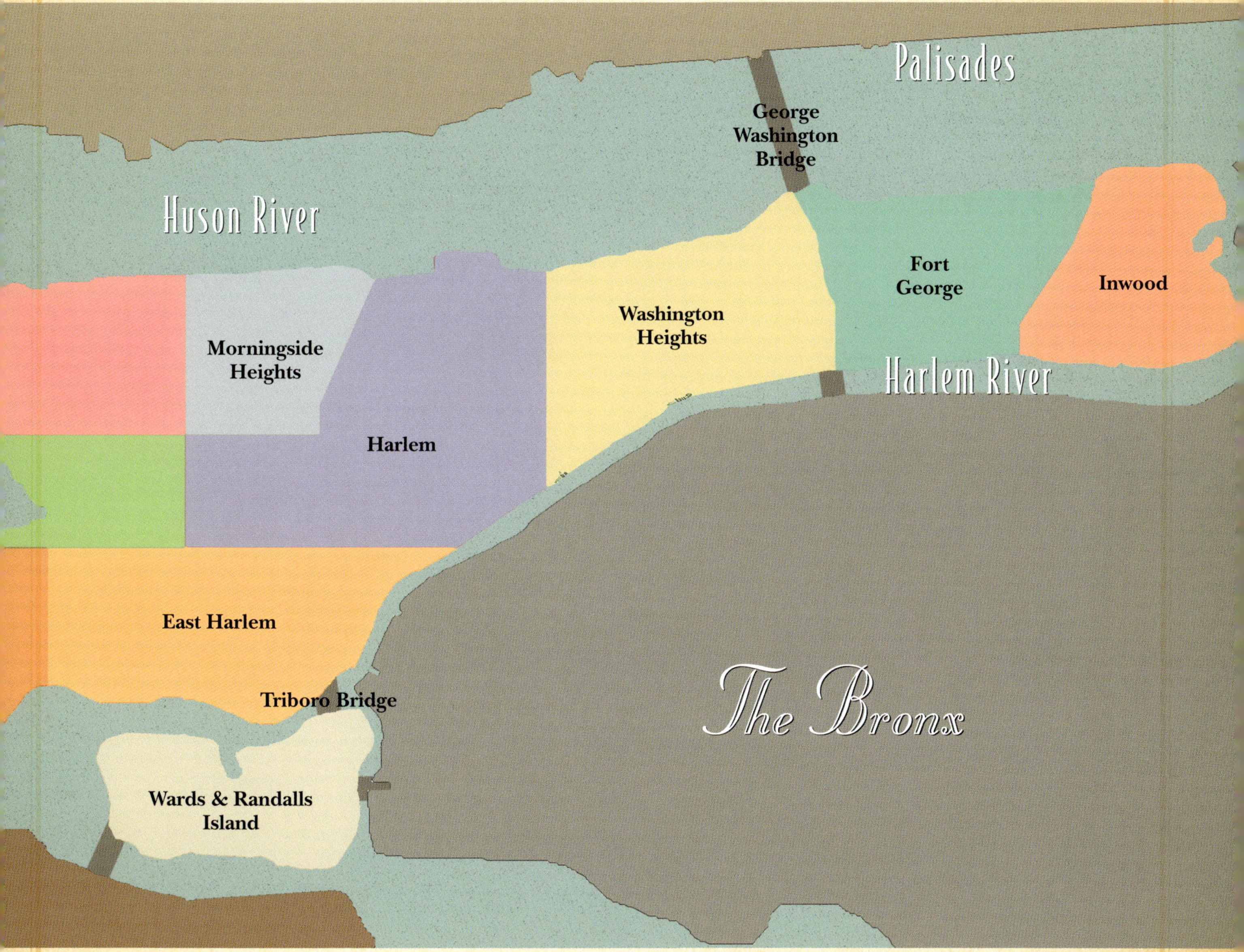
Palisades
George Washington Bridge
Huson River
Fort George
Inwood
Washington Heights
Morningside Heights
Harlem River
Harlem
East Harlem
Triboro Bridge
The Bronx
Wards & Randalls Island

To the Landmarks Preservation Commission and those who have fought to preserve the beauty of New York City: Thank you!